COCHRANE

FEB -- 2012

# COW

## A BOVINE BIOGRAPHY

**FLORIAN WERNER**

*Translated from the German by*
DORIS ECKER

GREYSTONE BOOKS

D&M PUBLISHERS INC.

Vancouver/Toronto/Berkeley

Greystone Books
An imprint of D&M Publishers Inc.
2323 Quebec Street, Suite 201
Vancouver BC Canada V5T 4S7
www.greystonebooks.com

Cataloguing data available from Library and Archives Canada
ISBN 978-1-55365-581-7 (pbk.) · ISBN 978-1-55365-980-8 (ebook)

Editing by Iva Cheung
Cover design by Peter Cocking
Every effort has been made to trace ownership of visual and written material
used in this book. Errors or omissions will be corrected in subsequent
printings, provided notification is sent to the publisher.
Unless credited to an English-language publication in the notes,
all translations of quotations are by Doris Ecker.
Printed and bound in Canada by Friesens
Text printed on acid-free paper
Distributed in the U.S. by Publishers Group West

The photograph of David Lynch's *Eat My Fear* on page 68
was generously provided by Färgfabriken, Stockholm.

The translation of this work was supported by a grant from the Goethe-Institut,
which is funded by the German Ministry of Foreign Affairs.

We gratefully acknowledge the financial support of the Canada Council
for the Arts, the British Columbia Arts Council, the Province of British Columbia
through the Book Publishing Tax Credit, and the Government of Canada
through the Canada Book Fund for our publishing activities.

# CONTENTS

# FOREWORD

IN THIS bovine biography, Florian Werner offers readers a fascinating literary perspective on the cow. His thorough research into cows' role in human culture has unearthed countless examples of the cow as a mother figure in literature, mythology, and religion. A major theme throughout this book is that cows have a symbiotic relationship with humans—one that has developed over thousands of years and that is mutually beneficial to both species. Humans breed, feed, and house cows, and in return they give us milk, meat, and other products.

In my own work with cattle, I've done some long, hard thinking about the relationship between humans and animals. My first contact with cows was in high school, where I learned how to milk cows at the school's small twelve-cow dairy. During the summer I visited my aunt's ranch in Arizona, and I was introduced to wild beef cattle that grazed on extensive pastures. Since these animals were not tame, they had to be held in a squeeze chute for their vaccinations. I saw that the pressure applied by the equipment had a calming effect on the animals. I became very interested in the squeeze chute because I was extremely anxious and had many panic attacks; my nervous system abnormalities, due to autism, made me desperate for relief. I tried getting in the cattle squeeze chute, and it calmed my nerves. This experience motivated me to design better equipment to handle the wild beef cattle that were not accustomed to close human contact. Since the 1970s, I have designed equipment for handling cattle in large slaughter plants; today half the cattle in the U.S. and Canada are handled in systems I developed. I discovered that if I eliminated little visual distractions within the system, such as reflections off shiny metal, a change in flooring texture, or a dangling chain, the cattle would walk peacefully up the chute to be killed. They were afraid of sensory detail that people often fail to notice.

After I had completed the design of one of my systems in 1990, I stood on a catwalk that looked over a sea of cattle. Realizing that they were going to die in a center track restrainer, a piece of equipment that I had developed, I became upset and began crying. But then I thought, "None of the cattle would have even existed if people had not bred and raised them." This fundamental truth makes regular appearances in this book. As Florian Werner notes, "It was only by letting themselves be domesticated by humans that [cows] could rise to be the most widespread and numerous large mammal on earth. They paid the price of freedom for a symbiotic relationship with humans and were thus protected from the dangers and burdens of life in the wild."

Because of my close work with animals, people ask me all the time if I eat meat. Yes, I do, and I eat beef often. I once tried a vegan diet but became so lightheaded that I couldn't function. I believe that my metabolism requires meat, and given that, as Werner shows, cows and humans have evolved together, depending on one another for millennia, I don't think it's too far-fetched to conclude that some people are just genetically predetermined to need to eat meat.

But since we breed the cattle for their meat and their milk, we owe them a decent life—one that is free of abuse and that offers them opportunities to have some positive experiences, like being able to live at least part of their lives on pasture. Scientific research makes it very clear that mammals experience negative emotions, such as fear and separation distress. Studies also show that they can experience positive emotions as well. That cows have feelings is clearly demonstrated in Florian Werner's careful selection of examples from our cultural history.

As I read Werner's numerous descriptions of cows in mythology and folk tales about cows, I was struck by how many of them were about individual animals rather than the herd. Individual cows have personalities, and the milkmaids and the cowherds throughout history have had relationships with individual cows. When I was in graduate school, I milked cows at the university dairy. Certain cows stood out from the herd, making a name for themselves as either really friendly or very difficult. One cow in particular would kick me only if I forgot who she was when I put on the milking machine. She never kicked when I remembered who she was and when I put the machine on with the respect she was due.

Although, as Werner shows in the chapter "Evil Cows," cows have, in the past decade, been demonized by figures like Jeremy Rifkin as the source of global warming and the destruction of landscapes and ecosystems, I am buoyed by the recent growth of sustainable agricultural practices, including organic farming, that make the best use of livestock and that demonstrate once again that we need cattle as much as they need us. When grazing is done right, it can increase biodiversity in grasslands: the manure from the animals fertilizes the soil, and well-managed grazing lands provide habitat and watering sources for wildlife. Vast areas in Africa, Australia, South America, and the U.S. stand to benefit from modern rotational grazing practices, which can increase plant growth, improving the carbon cycle and benefiting the environment.

If we heed the advice of Bernard Rollin, a philosopher of animal ethics, the next phase in the progression of this recent agricultural awakening will be the reintroduction of the ethics of husbandry into large-scale animal agriculture, a move that will help us never forget that cows are beings and not merely commodities. If we always keep in mind that the symbiosis central to our relationship with cows must be mutually beneficial to both species, we will finally give them the respect they deserve, both collectively and as individuals. Florian Werner's *Cow* is an important step in this direction. His book is a fine tribute to this peaceful animal, and it pays homage to the pivotal relationship we have with cows that makes us who we are as humans—a relationship that we too often take for granted.

TEMPLE GRANDIN
Author of *Animals in Translation* and *Animals Make us Human*

# IN THE BEGINNING
## WAS THE COW

W HEN GOD made heaven and earth, day and night, and land and water, he created cattle first, and only then, after having prepared the fields and pastures, man and woman. "God blessed them," the biblical account of creation tells us, "saying, 'Be fruitful and multiply . . . and let them rule . . . over the cattle and over all the earth, and over every creeping thing that creeps on the earth.'" So when Adam and Eve stepped onto the planet, they were already surrounded by cows. Even the script through which this story is passed down starts, in a way, with the cow: the aleph, א, the first letter of the Hebrew alphabet, is a stylized version of a horned cow. The Greek alpha, α, which developed into our letter a, is also reminiscent of a frontal view of a cow rotated ninety degrees.

In other mythologies the cow plays an even more prominent and active role in world creation. The ancient Egyptians, for example, believed that the heavens above were really the womb of a gigantic divine cow—one that carried the sun god,

Ra, on its back and was the source of the fertile waters of the Nile. According to the pastoral African Fulbe tribe, the earth was created from a drop of milk that came from the udder of the primeval cow Itoori. Germanic mythology tells that the milk and warm tongue of a divine cow called Auðumbla ensured the survival of earth's first inhabitants.

Cows did indeed play an extraordinary role in the pre- and protohistory of humankind. They supplied milk, and thus the animal protein necessary for our nutrition, and after their death they provided fuel for lamps in the form of tallow. They were able to carry significantly heavier loads than humans and helped to work the farmlands as draft animals. Their hides were used to make waterproof clothing and tent walls, their bones for tool handles and sewing needles. The domestication of cattle almost ten thousand years ago freed us from having to undertake a tiring and dangerous hunt for every meal of fresh meat.

In short, cows played an instrumental part in allowing humankind to settle down and to gradually transition from the nomadic existence of hunters and gatherers to advanced sedentary civilizations. "I am now absolutely convinced," writes veterinarian and cow expert Michael Brackmann, "that it wasn't so much the invention of the wheel . . . that enabled *Homo sapiens* to create advanced civilizations but the domestication of cattle." American science critic Jeremy Rifkin seconds the idea: "Western civilization has been built, in part, on the back of the bull and the cow."

THE RELATIONSHIP between humans and cattle was (and is) indeed symbiotic. Cattle submitted to us, and in return we took them into our care, helped them find food, cared for them in sickness, and protected them from wild animals. Cattle helped humans develop advanced civilizations, and in turn human support allowed them to populate the whole planet.

Originally endemic to the area that today comprises Iran, Pakistan, and northwestern India, the aurochs, ancestor of our domesticated cattle, had by the end of the last ice age already spread through large parts of Eurasia, eventually arriving in North Africa. It was, however, only with human assistance that its descendants succeeded in reaching other continents. Since the beginning of the modern era, cows have been conquering the entire globe in the wake of European colonizers. On his second journey to America in 1494, Christopher Columbus brought the first cattle to the New World. Following the Spanish conquistadores and missionaries, cattle spread through Central and South America during the sixteenth century. In order to meet the British Empire's steadily growing appetite for beef, New Zealand and Australia were finally developed as pastureland in the nineteenth century.

Cattle have played a significant part in shaping the face of the earth as we know it. Cattle husbandry gave rise not only to Europe's cultivated landscape, with its constantly alternating farmlands, pastures, and forests, but also to the endless grasslands of North America and the erosion-threatened clear-cuts of Central and South America, where millions and millions of acres of tropical rain forest had to make way for cattle pastures. Deliberately developed as cattle habitat, these areas were actively shaped by the hooves and mouths of those animals. That's why Jeremy Rifkin argues that humankind is no longer earth's subjugator, as the biblical account of creation suggests, but that we are rather up against an "imperium of cattle." Close to 1.3 billion exemplars of the species graze the earth today. Almost one quarter of the continental mass is used to supply them with grass and feed grain. Cattle are the most abundant group of large mammals in the earth's entire history. Their total weight amounts to more than double that of the human population.

The reason cattle spread on such a massive scale lies ultimately in their versatility. Cows supply us not only with labor, milk, meat, hide, and bones; the rest of their body parts and secretions are used as well. The German folk song "von Herrn Pasturn sien Kauh" (About the parson's cow), for example, praises the cow's universal endowments rather succinctly. Every verse is dedicated to a part of the physical legacy of a recently deceased cow and the respective beneficiaries of the products. The gracious parson gives every member of his congregation a piece of the cow carcass:

> And for the olde fire brigade
> a pot of axle grease is made
>
> And night watchman Father Thorn
> is blowing on his brand-new horn
>
> And the lowly butcher's boy
> all the guts will he employ
>
> Hey, sing, sing along now
> about the parson's cow

The fact that this song survives with hundreds of different verses gives an inkling of just how many things can be made from the remains of a cow. Tallow is an important base for soap, ointment, lipstick, and other cosmetics and in the past was used as wheel and machine grease—and apparently also for fire brigade vehicles. Cow horns are used for combs and piano keys and, although rarely today, for drinking horns and bugles. Guts are made into sausage casings—for example, for the popular Swiss cervelat. Cartilage is used in plastic surgery, whereas eyes end up in the stomachs of gourmets or on biology class dissecting tables. Even the cow's excrement comes in useful: cow pies are used as fertilizer or dried for fuel, and in the past, nitric acid, an ingredient in the production of gun powder, was extracted from cow urine. The standard corny joke that makes the rounds in the meat industry is that all parts of a cow are processed, except her moo.

THE COW has played a special role in humans' lives for thousands of years, be it as vital livestock or in the form of one of its countless products. So it's hardly surprising that time and again we have interpreted our existence in relation to cows. The above-mentioned creation stories, as well as countless other myths, fairy tales, novels, poems, plays, films, and paintings are populated with cows and illustrate the dynamic relationship between humans and cattle. Commercials for milk, cheese, or chocolate are inconceivable without cows. Even our everyday language abounds with metaphors, idioms, and sayings that refer to our millennia-long experience with these great creatures. When something or someone fails to materialize for a seemingly endless stretch of time, we feel we are condemned to wait "till the cows come home." "Don't have a cow" is the advice given to someone who gets too worked up about something. In German, a man marrying a pregnant woman would in the past have been told disapprovingly that he was "taking the cow with the calf." When Francophones experience something unexpected, they are likely to react with a surprised "*La vache!*" while Anglophones prefer the exclamation "Holy cow!"

One way or another, cows have over time come to occupy not only large parts of our globe but also our culture, our language, and our minds. Traditionally symbols of affluence, cows constituted the first natural currency, and we owe the most fundamental principles of capitalism (not to mention the word "capitalism" itself) to cattle husbandry. Believed to have grazed in the Garden of Eden, these quiet, reassuring, and peaceful animals are also a permanent fixture in our utopian imagination. It's almost impossible to imagine an ideal society or a pastoral idyll without some grazing cows in the background. As livestock that demand a lot of work to rear, they've been essential in shaping our relationship with nature—or, rather, with our "second," culturally modified nature. Author and journalist Eckhard Fuhr argues that values like sustainability, durability, and diligence were only introduced into agriculture when dairy farming was established. That industry imposed the need for careful cattle husbandry and handling of that precious, perishable udder secretion—milk. Cow's milk has functioned as "a kind of governess . . . It can be conserved only in accordance with, not against, nature."

BECAUSE OF this longstanding close relationship between humans and cattle, the cow has virtually become a member of the human family. "The relationship between a mountain dweller and his cows constitutes a genuine mutual exchange of appreciation," travel writer Johann Gottfried Ebel wrote in 1798 in his *Schilderung der Gebirgsvölker der Schweitz* (Portrait of the mountain peoples of Switzerland). "The cow gives him everything he requires; in return, the Alpine dairyman cares for and loves it, sometimes more than his children." According to Ebel, there even was the odd Alpine dairyman who kept his animals "cleaner than himself" and who chose the remedies for his sick cow "more carefully and cautiously than for his sick wife."

Within the hierarchy of domestic animals the cow has, at least in the Western world, always been somewhat overshadowed by the horse. The latter is a prestigious animal, once used to ride into battle, while the cow just got to pull the camp follower's cart behind the front lines, if she wasn't left in the shed altogether. That's why the cow has a pleasantly unmilitary, even pacifist, image—she is a civilian. She stays at home with the women and children, matching, in a way, the traditional image of women in patriarchal societies. In contrast to the horse, with its bellicose, male connotations, the cow is the preserver. She stands for normality, for everyday life; she generates offspring and food. The Germanic earth-mother goddess Nerthus chose, according to the Roman historian Tacitus, not fiery steeds but cows to draw her wagon across the country, bringing peace to every place she traveled.

And other remarkable parallels exist between women and cows. They are, as Eckhard Fuhr puts it, connected by an "odd biological harmony." The fertility cycle of cows follows, like that of women, the phases of the moon, and pregnancy in humans and cows lasts almost equally long: both give birth to the fruit of their womb after approximately forty weeks.

Because of these cultural and biological similarities, the cow is sometimes considered almost human, to the point where the boundaries between cattle and humans—and above all, between cows and women—are nearly dissolved. We've seen this theme time and again, especially in literature.

ALTHOUGH COWS are omnipresent in our lives, thought, and speech, and despite the attempts of more than a few writers to put themselves into their horned heads, cows have continued to puzzle us. Cows are inscrutable and extremely contradictory creatures and as such have challenged us into construing the most conflicting interpretations of their character. There is hardly a domestic animal that has engendered so many and such varied opinions as the cow. Depending on culture, epoch, and personal point of view, she is considered beautiful or ugly, divine or mundane, wise or mad, as a maternal animal or as an object of desire, as a sensitive creature or, in the words of Robert Musil, as "grazing beef."

In ancient Greece, for example, the expression "cow-eyed" was a flattering epitaph for the gracious goddess Hera; today it would hardly do as a compliment for a woman. Many people think of cows as dumb; expressions such as "stupid cow" or the German "*Rindvieh*" (cattle) are considered insults. The philosopher Friedrich Nietzsche, however, praised cows as the epitome of perfect worldly happiness. Cartoonists such as Gary Larson prefer to portray cows as figures of fun, while other artists are rather more fascinated by the melancholy cows exude: "*Les vaches*," writes the French poet Frédéric Boyer, "*sont notre object de mélancolie*." In the end, the individual beholders will decide which ideas, aversions, and desires they want to project onto the cow, what they believe to see in her, and how they portray her. The cow is the sum of all our narratives about her; or, as the philosopher Bruno Latour puts it: "There is no such thing as an objective image of the cow."

The cow is a human invention in yet another, very different respect. Up to about ten thousand years ago, there were, simply put, only two different kinds of cattle: firstly, *Bos*

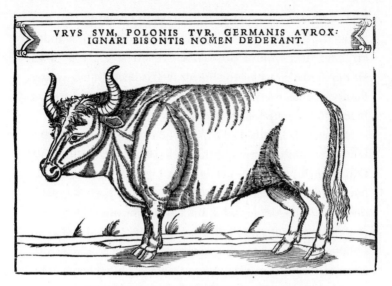

VRVS SVM, POLONIS TVR, GERMANIS AVROX:
IGNARI BISONTIS NOMEN DEDERANT.

Sigismund von Herberstein's illustration of an aurochs,
ancestor of modern cattle (1556). The caption reads, "I'm ursus,
in Polish *tur*, in German *aurox*: the unlearned call me bison."

*primigenius primigenius*, commonly known as aurochs or urus, considered to be the ancestor of today's Western cattle breeds. It was, as Caesar described (with slight exaggeration) in *The Gallic Wars*, almost as big as an elephant and equipped with mighty "strength and nimbleness," although that did not prevent it from being driven to extinction by humans. The last specimen died in Poland in 1627. Secondly, there is *Bos primigenius namadicus*, the so-called Asian aurochs, endemic to the Indian subcontinent and also extinct today. It evolved into the Indian domestic cattle breed zebus.

Among these two breeds of urus, there were presumably already several subgenera that had adapted to their respective ecological, climatological, and geographical circumstances.

It was, however, human intervention in breeding that produced the diverse spectrum of cattle breeds we know today. Michael Brackmann postulates that there are around six hundred different cattle breeds in existence. Dutch painter Marleen Felius even records more than a thousand different breeds in her encyclopedia *Cattle Breeds*.

Many of these breeds are threatened with extinction by the increasing globalization, industrialization, and monopolization of cattle breeding—in Germany, for example, four breeds constitute 97 percent of all cows, although there's greater diversity in the Alpine states. But it would be overly simplistic, if not presumptuous, to talk about *the* cow. After all, what do lightweight Dahomey miniature cattle have in common with Angus cows that outweigh them threefold? What connection is there between velvet-skinned, Bardot-eyed Jersey cows and shaggy Scottish Highland cattle? Or between high-volume milk producers like Holsteins and Limousins, which are bred exclusively for their meat; to say nothing of the white cows in England's Chillingham Park, whose sole raison d'être is to serve as an aesthetic showpiece for humans?

It is, however, pretty safe to say this much: all of these radically different creatures are ruminants of the cattle genus that communicate through sounds we refer to as mooing and that are generally considered good-natured and peaceable. The latter, however, doesn't apply to steers or bulls, and that point is key: the cow is female. Steers and bulls (that is, sexually mature male cattle) or oxen (castrated male cattle) will make only a cameo appearance in this book. Impressive because of their proverbial virility and indispensable in events like bullfighting or rodeos and for the production of oxtail soup, they play—compared with cows—an inferior role, economically as well as culturally speaking. To us as "herd proprietors," the bovine is, as Johann Wolfgang von Goethe observed, "significant only in terms of reproduction and nutrition, of milk and calves." In both instances, the male is only marginally involved.

The focal point of this book is thus the maternal, milk-giving, gentle, approachable, and seemingly familiar cow. The individual chapters are each dedicated to an important aspect of the coexistence of humans and cows. They focus, among other things, on cows as commodities, as suppliers of meat and milk, as sexual objects, as advertising media, as saints and devils, as slaves, as soul comforters, and as a danger to the environment. We'll ask what cows are trying to tell us when they moo, why milk is proof of the existence of God, and whether good cows go to heaven when they die. What exactly those cows look like—whether they are two-toned like black-and-white Holsteins or rather more monochrome like Swiss brown cows, whether they have humps like Indian zebus or curved horns like Hungarian longhorns—is left to the reader's taste and imagination.

# A KINGDOM FOR A COW

IN 1968 American comedian Pat Paulsen ran for president. In one of his best-known campaign speeches he tried to explain different political systems by using a series of glib examples like the ones found in economics textbooks. Paulsen's examples all started with the same premise: "You have two cows." What subsequently happened to those two cows quickly revealed the advantages, but mostly the disadvantages, of different political ideologies.

SOCIALISM: You have two cows; you give one to your neighbor.

COMMUNISM: You have two cows; the government takes both and gives you some milk.

FASCISM: You have two cows; the government takes both and sells you the milk.

NAZISM: You have two cows; the government takes both and shoots you.

NEW DEALISM: You have two cows; the government takes both, shoots one, milks the other and throws part of the milk down the sink.

CAPITALISM: You have two cows; you sell one and buy a bull.

Since the underlying principle of this sketch can be expanded almost arbitrarily, dozens of different versions of Paulsen's economic cow allegory are now in circulation. These versions may well vary substantially from each other, but they all share the same punch line: only the capitalist is unencumbered by half-baked ideologies and does the obvious. He makes sure that the number of his milk- and value-add-producing cattle increases. By purchasing a mate for the cow, he creates the foundations of what Jeremy Rifkin calls an "imperium of cattle." Considering all the stupid and cruel things that socialists, communists, and other political fanatics are supposedly doing to their cows, the actions of the capitalist seem soothingly pragmatic, even natural.

It's hardly surprising that capitalism wins out in this joke. After all, the cow is the capitalist animal par excellence. It's no accident that in colloquial German the word *Kuhhandel* (cow trade) describes a type of murky barter in the course of which one party, usually the buyer, is cheated. The cow is ideally suited for such dodgy deals, as it takes a long time to find out how well she really performs. You can take a horse for a sample ride. It's easy to tell whether a pig is meaty if you give its haunch a good pinch. It's a lot harder, especially for amateurs, to determine how much milk a cow will yield and whether she'll be suitable as a draft animal in the long run. In the Brothers Grimm fairytale "Hans in Luck," the protagonist learns this the hard way when he sells his cow and trades down repeatedly until he is finally without any possessions whatsoever. In this case, the seller is the one who comes to grief for a change:

> "Your cow will give you no milk: don't you see she is an old beast, good for nothing but the slaughter-house? . . . To please you I will change, and give you my fine fat pig for the cow."
>
> "Heaven reward you for your kindness and self-denial!" said Hans, as he gave the butcher the cow; and taking the pig off the wheel-barrow, drove it away, holding it by the string that was tied to its leg.

The cow is of course worth far more than the puny piglet. But "lucky" Hans, who has no clue about animals or commercial transactions, naively trusts the cunning butcher's judgment. It would seem that the cattle trade does indeed lend itself to leaving one's trading partner in the dark about the commodity's exact value and to making a maximum profit. In other words, cattle trading is the epitome of market-based trading. One could even say that our predominant form of economy would be inconceivable without cows.

BECAUSE OF their tremendous importance as draft animals and producers of milk, meat, and leather, cows have been synonymous with wealth in large parts of the Western world for thousands of years. If you owned cows, you were considered affluent. If you could afford only one cow, you at least didn't have to live in fear of starvation. As an old German saying goes, "a cloak and a cow cover up a lot of poverty." In many European languages, expressions relating to private property and the world of finance are often deeply rooted in the world of cattle trading. The Old High German word *feo* refers to both "*Vieh*" (cattle) and "*väterliches Gut*" (paternal property); the second meaning still exists in today's English as the word "fee." The adjective "pecuniary," as well as the vernacular German "*Penunze*" (money) are derived from the Latin word for money, *pecunia*, which in turn goes back to the word for cattle, *pecus*. Much more frequently used and so fundamental for the market economy, the word "capital" has the same root as the word "cattle": both are derived from the Latin *caput*, "head." In Roman times, someone who could call many heads his own—who, in other words, owned a large number of cows— was, in the original sense of the word, a capitalist.

Although owning many heads of cattle is nowadays by no means equivalent to being rich, the appreciation of the cow as a special asset lives on in our late-capitalist society. In the field of business economics, for example, the expression "cash cow" denotes an established product that yields stable earnings. It sits quietly in the homey company shed, requiring but modest investment, and can therefore be milked with profit. When the German newspaper *Süddeutsche Zeitung* announced the expansion of its business section at the beginning of 2008, the ad didn't feature a bull, the traditional symbol for a rising stock market, but a cow. The image of the bronze bull statue seen at all big stock exchanges worldwide had been digitally altered to include an udder, with a milk bucket at the ready underneath. The image seems to suggest that for clever investors the important question is not whether it's a bull market or whether the shares are rising. What's crucial is to have enough cash cows. Dairy cows may not be as strong and profitable as bulls, but they are far more predictable.

The cover of Bill Catlette and Richard Hadden's
book *Contented Cows Give Better Milk* (1998).

The cow, however, symbolizes more than stable profits. It
also stands for the employees who generate these earnings.
In 1998, a popular guide to business management published
in the U.S. featured a punctiliously dressed cow in a suit and
tie on its cover. The title read, *Contented Cows Give Better Milk*.
The basic message of the book is that managers should treat
their employees as well as farmers treat their dairy cattle—
and not just for some ridiculous ethical reason but because
only then will the employees develop to their full potential.
The book spawned a sequel less than ten years later, *Contented Cows Moove Faster*, a title that implies that happy "human

resources" not only produce better-quality work but also work more efficiently. The author didn't seem to mind that the consistent bovinization of two-legged employees carries unhuman undertones.

Another reason cows have played such a vital role in the evolution of capitalism is their mobility. Not only were cows extremely valuable, but they also constituted one of the first forms of movable property, a chattel that could be herded from A to B and then offered for barter in many cultures. As a generally known and relatively constant economic entity, cows were used as a point of reference for barter. Otto Schrader writes: "Herd animals, and dairy cows in particular, are the oldest value indicator among Indo-Germanic peoples." So cows were a predecessor of the concept of currency. They could be used as a means of payment.

According to accounts in Greek mythology, for example, the god Mercury buys the silence of the only witness to his cattle theft, the aged Battus, with "a gleaming heifer." The practice seems to have been so common in those days that Old Greek had an idiom for it: "A cow has been put onto my tongue," meaning, more or less, "I've been bribed with a cow and so can't speak freely."

As Sir Walter Scott relates in his novel *Waverley*, cows were held as pawn in eighteenth-century Scotland to push claims for outstanding cash settlements:

> He that steals a cow from a poor widow, or a stirk from a cottar, is a thief; he that lifts a drove from a Sassenach laird is a gentleman-rover.

Even today, cows serve as a symbolic currency in many African cultures. When South African president Thabo Mbeki failed to make an appearance at the wedding of the king of Lesotho, he was "fined" by the king and promptly paid up: the following spring he presented the king with a magnificent Holstein cow.

In these cases, cows constitute a natural currency, the original form of money per se. What makes natural currencies special is that, unlike shells, coins, banknotes, or credit cards, they have a practical and a symbolic value. As Karl Marx put it, they have a use value as well as an exchange value. In contrast to a thousand-dollar bill, a cow can be milked, slaughtered, and skinned; that's her use value. However—assuming you live in a society that accepts cows as a currency—you can also use a cow as an intermediate means of barter, a placeholder and symbolic equivalent for another service or commodity; that's her exchange value.

According to Marx, the exchange value subsequently assumes an increasingly independent existence. It is indeed more powerful than the practical use of the commodity. As a result the commodity takes on a so-called fetish character. It's no longer judged on whether we really need it, but it appears as a magical object, the graven image of a primitive natural religion. It turns into the proverbial golden calf to whom human sacrifices must be offered if needed. In this case, the purpose of work is no longer to produce use value but, above all, to earn an increase in exchange value—that is, to make a profit.

According to the Roman writer Tacitus, people began turning the natural currency cow into a commodity fetish very early on. In his first-century CE treatise *Germania*, he gives an account of the barbaric two- and four-legged inhabitants north of the Alps:

It is well provided with live-stock; but the animals are mostly undersized, and even the cattle lack the handsome heads that are their natural glory. It is the mere number of them that the Germans take pride in; for these are the only form of wealth they have and are much prized. Silver and gold have been denied them—whether of divine favor or of divine wrath, I cannot say . . . The natives take less pleasure than most people in possessing and handling these metals.

To the Romans, who used precious metals such as silver and gold as symbolic means of barter, it seemed incomprehensible that the Teutons were so devoted to their cows, seeing as the animals were slight and ugly and didn't even show the pretty forehead skin pattern that the inhabitants of the Apennine Peninsula valued so much. And yet, the Teutons just couldn't get enough of them; "mere numbers" made them happy. And considering that cows constitute walking, grazing money (while silver and gold, as Tacitus remarked, played only a minor role in barter north of the Alps), the German forefathers' way of trading seems, at least from a late-capitalist perspective, quite consistent. Money doesn't have to be pretty, as long as there is plenty of it.

And if, as is the custom with cows who share a pasture with a bull, it even multiplies automatically—that is, if it generates "interest"—all the better. As interest-bearing capital, the cow reaches, to quote Marx again, its "most fetishist form." It develops a life of its own in which its practical use value recedes into the background. The cow is now reduced to its function of creating ever more natural currency; it is, as Marx would say, "money which begets money," or, rather, a cow-bearing cow. And, as such, cows have time and again managed to stimulate the kind of irrational desire that normally only "filthy lucre" can evoke.

Old Battus in Ovid's *Metamorphoses*, for example, could easily retire with his bribe, the cow that Mercury gave him. But no: owning the cow actually arouses his greed. When Mercury returns shortly after the cattle theft, looking different and disguising his voice in order to put the old man's silence to the test, Battus immediately divulges the whereabouts of the stolen cattle. After all, the supposed stranger offers to pay him with "a heifer—and a bull" for the confidential information. Battus can't resist the prospect of a "double bribe," especially since it may well multiply in the coming years without his doing anything. Unfortunately he is not allowed to enjoy the interest of his betrayal: to punish him for his breach of promise, Mercury turns Battus into stone.

In the novella *Die Kuh* (The cow) by the German poet Friedrich Hebbel, the greed for cattle also leads to catastrophe. The novella is set in an early-nineteenth-century smallholding. After years of hard work, the miserly but ambitious farmer Andreas, the story's tragic hero, has finally saved enough money to buy a cow. His wife and the farmhand, Hans, have gone to fetch the animal from the seller and close the deal. The farmer and his three-year-old son await their return in happy anticipation. His dream is about to come true. In just a few moments he will be the proud owner of a cow.

> "Can you hear it bellow yet?" He jumped up and rushed to the window. "Not so," he said returning, "that came from the neighbor's shed! Well now, tomorrow the reply will come from my own shed! Well, my boy . . . Your father has

finally made it, the cow is already on its way! You have to get yourself a horse when you are grown up! You hear me?!"

To while away the waiting time, Andreas smugly looks at the money he has saved up for the purchase of this cow in the light of the tallow lamp, telling himself once more in detail the story of how he has earned it. He seems to be more devoted to the bills on the table in front of him than to his son, who is playing next to him.

When night slowly falls and neither his wife nor his farmhand have arrived with the cow, the farmer steps out to smoke his Sunday pipe in front of the door, leaving his son alone inside together with the burning lamp. A fatal error, as it turns out. The little boy doesn't yet understand the "true nature" of money. Through childish eyes he judges his father's bills by their practical value—as fuel for a fun spectacle when lit with the tallow lamp. When the farmer returns to the room, the last bill has just burned up.

In a blind rage, the farmer grasps his little son by the hair and hurls him against the wall, so that he lies "on the floor with his skull cracked and his brains spluttered about." He then takes the rope with which the cow was meant to be tethered, climbs up into the attic of the house and hangs himself. A few seconds later, his wife and the farmhand finally arrive with the eagerly anticipated cow. They, too, meet their death shortly. The farmer's wife faints at the sight of her slain son. The farmhand climbs up into the attic with the tallow lamp in his hand, runs into the farmer's dead body, falls backwards off the ladder, and breaks his neck. The lamp sets the straw on fire, whereupon the whole house, including the unconscious farmer's wife, burns down until there is nothing left of the family but "shrunken skeletons." Not even the cow survives the catastrophe. "That much is sure," Hebbel concludes, "that the cow, following the ill-fated instinct of her kind, ran into the fire and burned to death with the rest of them."

The destructive consequences of capitalism have hardly ever been described more drastically and, in a narrative sense, "economically" than in this story—the whole tragedy is less than five pages long. The very moment the farmer gets the chance to move up in life and literally become a capitalist— that is, the owner of a head of cattle—catastrophe befalls him. The farmer is so blinded by the prospect of finally becoming his neighbor's equal through the purchase of such a prestigious and profitable animal that it totally warps his perspective. The life of his son seems, if only for a short-tempered moment, worth less than owning a cow. And when, after his son's death, he hears the "longed-for bellow" of the animal that he will never own, he decides that his own life too has become worthless. The cow's mooing "gives him the strength to make a sudden decision"—to commit suicide.

Everything that was meant for the cow has become an instrument of death. The bills for her purchase are the child's undoing. The rope intended to tether her is coiled around the farmer's neck. The ladder leading to the straw storage proves fatal for the farmhand. The straw on which the animal was supposed to have lain burns the farmer's wife to death. And the cow itself, the much desired fetish around which the whole tragedy revolves, destroys itself in the end. Every commodity is dependent on whether there is a market for it. If nobody is left to appreciate its value, it loses, from the market economy point of view, its right to exist.

IT'S SIGNIFICANT that the flashback to the actual bargain, the negotiations over the price for the fatal cloven-hoofed animal, constitutes one of the few comical moments of this otherwise somber and pessimistic story. When his wife stays away longer than anticipated, it's not so much the worry that something could have happened to her that bothers the farmer. What he's concerned about is that the seller of the cow might have made so much money in the bargain that he may have decided to invite his wife to dinner. Moments later, he speculates that his wife may have started haggling over the cow's price again. The farmer can, however, not fathom that anybody could possibly be a tougher negotiating partner than he himself. "Good luck, but hats off to he who manages to pinch off another penny where I struck a bargain!"

In moments like that, the farmer Andreas resembles less the tragic figure he is at the end of the day but more a character out of a comedy of errors: the miser; the disagreeable penny pincher; the pathological tightwad, who knows he's obsessed with money but is strangely proud of his obsession. Apart from Hebbel's story, the cattle trade is not usually the chosen topic of great tragedies but rather the stuff comedies are made from. In the first half of the twentieth century alone, at least half a dozen humorous popular plays and comedies emerged that mentioned cattle trading in the title.

On the one hand, this may have to do with the way that the dogged bargaining for cattle appeals more to the "lower" instincts like greed and deviousness rather than to the noble, heroic emotions that tragedy is traditionally devoted to. On the other hand, the people involved in the cattle trade can hardly be considered tragedy material. According to classic definitions of drama, the protagonists of comedies are more

likely to belong to the lower classes, while the heroes of tragedies are members of the highest social strata. A cow is of
course completely out of place in such an illustrious milieu. If,
however, she happens to stray into that kind of scenario, the
effect is inevitably comical.

The English-language version of Kurt Weill and Robert
Vambery's operetta *Der Kuhhandel*, for example, is entitled
*A Kingdom for a Cow*. The sentence is a play on words from the
famous scene in Shakespeare's dark royal drama *Richard III*.
The last words of the murderous eponymous hero, who has lost
his horse in battle and senses that his own life and kingdom
will soon come to an end, are: "A horse! A horse! My kingdom
for a horse!" By replacing the noble horse, the animal with
which medieval English kings rode into battle, with a mundane peasant cow, the English translators of the Weill operetta
hint at the fact that the operetta will turn out to be a lot less
woeful and bloody than Shakespeare's tragedy. A general who,
booted and spurred, sword at the ready, rides into battle on
the back of a cow is, as the playbill of the London Savoy Theatre illustrates, not a sight that would inspire fear in a military
opponent.

Although *A Kingdom for a Cow* does involve political intrigue,
war, treason, and the mother country, the wedding plans of
sweethearts Juan and Juanita are at the center of the action.
Their plan fails repeatedly because their cow—the lovers' only
livelihood and dowry—gets taken away from them. On the
very evening before the planned wedding, the president of the
fictitious banana republic Santa Maria, where they live, suddenly enacts a so-called welfare tax in order to increase the
military prowess of his country. Since Juan can't pay the tax,
the bailiff confiscates his cow. Juan, however, doesn't give up

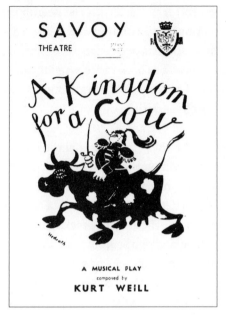

Playbill from the Savoy Theatre's production of
*A Kingdom for a Cow* by Kurt Weill (1935).

but persistently works long hours until he has enough money for a new cow. He and Juanita are already kneeling at the altar, when the bailiff makes a second appearance and takes away the new cow as the next welfare tax installment. To make matters worse, Juan is drafted, and a murderous automatic weapon takes the place of the peaceful cow that promised affluence and marital bliss:

> I used to have a splendid cow,
> The cow is long since dead,
> And now I have, oh help me Lord,
> A hefty gun instead.

It's only when the arms race with the neighboring country ends and the American capitalist who delivered weapons to the two enemy states has been exposed as a war-monger that Juan and Juanita can buy back the cow and the three exchange marriage vows: "I am yours and you are mine," they sing, "and the cow belongs to us both."

NOWADAYS IT'S hard to imagine that the happiness of two lovers should depend on the possession of a cow. In the old days, however, owning dairy cattle used to be seen as a sign of economic independence and could well be a prerequisite for starting a household. The ancient Greeks gave their daughters names that hinted at a rich four-legged inheritance and were meant to lure potential spouses or sons-in-law—for example, Polyboea, "she who has many cows," or Phereboia, "she who will bring many cows into the marriage." And even in early-twentieth-century rural Germany the broad back of a cow often smoothed the way into the marital bed. At least that's what Swabian playwright Hermann Essig suggests in his play *Die Glückskuh* (The lucky cow), which premiered in 1911.

The female hero of the comedy, Rebekkle Palmer, is attractive, funny, smart (or shrewd, at any rate)—and pregnant. Before her disgrace shows and becomes common knowledge in the village, she quickly has to find a bridegroom, and that's the problem. Although Rebekkle has many suitors, none of them is willing to marry her without dowry. Helm, her lover and the father of the child, stoically remarks that "it just isn't the done thing to marry one who has nothing." Manuel, a rich farmer's son, who is caught in her bedroom one night, is not allowed to lead the girl to the registry office either. "He has to find one who brings a cow into the marriage," Manuel's mother says at the beginning of the play. Later on, she remarks that a cow plainly and simply is the kind of dowry that "every farmer demands."

So Rebekkle knows what to do. She sneaks out of the family house, steals a cow in the neighboring village and triumphantly returns just as the village starts gossiping about her alleged lewd behavior. In view of the dowry she has in tow, the villagers' attitudes change abruptly. "Rebekkle with a real cow," the bystanders marvel. "Why don't you stay here with your cow?" "Put her into our cowshed for now." "Do you know how to handle a cow by yourself?" When Rebekkle announces that the cow at her side is really a "double cow"—that is, a cow that will soon calve—the greedy mouths of Manuel's family immediately start watering. Manuel is told to marry Rebekkle right away.

It doesn't seem to bother him or his parents that he will get "the cow with the calf" not only in the literal but also in the proverbial sense of the old German expression—that is, he's marrying a pregnant woman. A veritable race begins: Manuel simply has to be the first to get the bride into the marital bed and the cow into the family shed. "You are taking too much time, and then someone else will take a liking to the cow," the mayor reprimands the newly engaged couple, as they run toward the village hall to tie the knot. "Can't the cow run a bit more quickly?" It almost seems as if Manuel is to marry the cow, not the woman.

Rebekkle, too, knows that her attractiveness as a bride waxes and wanes with the cow as a dowry. So she kisses first the cow, then the groom, when Manuel proposes to her. "Oh my dear little cow! . . . Oh my good Manuel." The happiness that the cow brings about is indeed short-lived. When it becomes apparent that the "double cow" was stolen and therefore can't be considered dowry, Manuel's family insists that the marriage be promptly annulled. One shady bargain follows another until Rebekkle's marriage deal is finally signed, sealed, and delivered. And, as is customary for a comedy, a wedding can take place—this time with Helm, the child's father.

The bitter irony of it all is of course that the potential husbands scramble to get their hands on the cow in calf, while nobody really wants to have the pregnant bride. The male characters in "The Lucky Cow" view female sexuality mostly through an economic lens. Although they are familiar with the bovine life cycle, the gentlemen actually have no idea about female biology. "You know all about your cow," Rebekkle reproaches the guileless Helm, when he totally fails to understand what is happening to her, "but you look at me as if this were a wonder." Little wonder, in fact, as a calf brings money; an out-of-wedlock child, by contrast, brings disgrace and costs alimony. Up until now, Helm has obviously been dealing mostly with breeding cows.

As in many other comedies, the central motif in "The Lucky Cow" is the corrupting influence of money, or, in this case, of cows. Under the spell of the natural currency, the villagers are capable of unpredictable depravity as well as surprising affirmations of love. All of their social interactions, even their seemingly authentic feelings, are driven entirely by greed and have been perverted by the sudden appearance of the cow. "Money," writes Karl Marx, "transforms loyalty into treason, love into hate, hate into love, . . . reason into nonsense." In view of all the trials and tribulations that the new capital has brought to the village, Helm states in act four that he is fed up with cows: "What is a cow after all? It makes you disloyal." It may well be an important status symbol and a precious dowry, but the fact remains: a cow can't buy happiness.

# FLESH AND BLOOD

IN THE second volume of his five-part novel about the life and heroic deeds of the giants Gargantua and Pantagruel, French Renaissance poet François Rabelais gives an account of the tremendous hunger that Pantagruel, the younger of the two, is said to have felt right after his birth. He allegedly imbibed the milk of 17,913 cows with each meal, handling the animals as carelessly as other children treat their feeding bottles. Human wet nurses were incapable of satisfying the newborn's appetite. Very soon, however, even those huge quantities of milk were no longer enough for Pantagruel:

> One day in the morning, when they would have made him suck one of his cows . . . , he got óne of his arms loose from the swaddling bands wherewith he was kept fast in the cradle, laid hold on the said cow under the left foreham, and grasping her to him ate up her udder and half of her paunch, with the liver and the kidneys, and had devoured all up if she had not cried out most

Gustave Doré's illustration of Pantagruel feeding (1854).

horribly . . . at which noise company came in and took away the said cow from Pantagruel. Yet could they not so well do it but that the quarter whereby he caught her was left in his hand, of which quarter he gulped up the flesh in a trice, even with as much ease as you would eat a sausage . . . and afterwards began fumblingly to say, Good, good, good—for he could not yet speak plain—giving them to understand thereby that he had found it very good, and that he did lack but so much more.

To this day, the French language honors his memory: if someone is a voracious eater, that person is said to have *un appétit pantagruélique.*

Even though Pantagruel is a grotesquely exaggerated literary figure and his legendary appetite will hardly find its equal in the real world, Rabelais's giant does have a few things in common with today's average human meat eater. He craves beef. He likes eating it raw. He demonstrates, by eating this kind of food, his special power. And, he is a man.

AMONG ALL food, beef has, as Jeremy Rifkin has observed, the highest status. In almost all meat-eating cultures, red meat is held in the highest esteem, followed by poultry and fish, then animal products such as eggs, milk, and cheese, and finally—at the very bottom of the nutritional pyramid— vegetables, fruit, and grains. A country's beef consumption usually grows in parallel with its GDP. Rifkin consequently argues that being part of "the world's most exclusive beef club" defines a nation's geopolitical status as clearly as "the number of its tanks and ships or the rise in its industrial output."

And what holds true for entire nations also holds true for their citizens. Those who can afford it order prime rib or rib eye steak at a restaurant. The less well-heeled go for pork chops or half a chicken. Vegetable patties and salads are mostly left to women. Western men eat about 60 percent more meat than women and twice the amount of meat products.

That's why most of the attributes assigned to beef and its consumers have male connotations.

Beef is supposed to make you strong, aggressive, and passionate, which is why in the old days pubescent boys were often deprived of it. A vegetarian diet was believed to be the best weapon against masturbation. Conversely, soldiers, who were expected to be particularly manly and combative in battle, were virtually crammed with beef. In the eighteenth century, British seafarers received an annual allowance of a whopping 95 kilograms (210 pounds). And the deserving army veterans who guard the Tower of London are to this day referred to as Beefeaters, presumably because they were traditionally given larger beef rations than other members of the royal household. The idea that beef makes people particularly argumentative lives on in English in the expression "to have a beef with someone."

Evidently even today the premise holds true: if you want to make it in our paternalistic society, you should eat beef. "In our countries, who would stand any chance of becoming a chef d'Etat (head of state)," the French philosopher Jacques Derrida asked, "by publicly . . . declaring him- or herself to be a vegetarian? The chef has to be an eater of flesh." In the early 1970s, McDonald's Japan boss Den Fujita speculated, much to the displeasure of his American interview partner, that the persistent consumption of minced beef could change anyone into a conquest-mad "Aryan." "If we eat hamburgers for a thousand years, we will become blond. And when we become blond we can conquer the world."

WE MIGHT have to take this last statement with a grain of salt, but it still demonstrates what beef symbolizes, not just in the Western world, but even in the Far East: physical strength, a thirst for power and superiority. The reason beef is so highly appreciated has less to do with its actual nutritional value (in fact, eating less meat would be healthier for most people) and more with its symbolic nature. Even at the beginning of human history the consumption of dead animals was likely perceived as a sign of special strength and power. Meat expert Nan Mellinger speculates that this association is partially due to the fact that hunting for prey was originally accompanied by the fear of becoming the victim. If you killed a wild animal in the Neolithic period, it might have been in self-defense at first. If you returned victoriously with your animal prey, you had triumphed in a life-and-death struggle.

The need to defend oneself accompanied a growing human urge to ingest the opponent's power in a quasi-cannibalistic manner by eating its flesh. After all, "You are what you eat." By eating the flesh of a recently killed aurochs, for example, the hunter hoped to acquire the animal's tremendous physical strength. And what was right for stone-age cave dwellers is proper for today's gourmets. "Steak," writes Roland Barthes about the French national dish, "is a part of the same sanguine mythology as wine. It is the heart of meat, it is meat in its pure state, and whoever partakes of it assimilates a bull-like strength . . . Full-bloodedness is the raison d'être of the steak."

It's significant that Barthes brings the notion of blood into play—it is, after all, the elixir that allegedly gives dark beef its special powers. When in Bertolt Brecht's radical teaching play *Saint Joan of the Stockyards* Chicago "meat king" and über-capitalist Pierpont Mauler suddenly feels pangs of remorse as he sees the destitute masses and starts showing signs of human feelings, his partner immediately decides to serve him a bloody steak as a remedy: "I'll force a raw steak on him. His old weakness has hit him again. Maybe eating raw meat will bring him to his senses." Swiss writer Beat Sterchi tells a similar story in his novel *The Cow*, where a butcher's apprentice drinks the powerful lifeblood of his first "victim" in a quasi initiation rite. "The first time he slaughters a cow himself, he cups his hands and drinks from her veins so that she'll live on in me."

Most avid meat eaters would probably recoil from such an archaic libation; but even they usually prefer their steak bloody or at best medium rare, because it is in this form that it most resembles the raw natural state of freshly slaughtered cattle. The blood that seeps from the steak every time you stab it with a fork or cut it with a knife is reminiscent of the act of killing. As Nan Mellinger puts it, the idea of power has "in the history of mankind always [been linked] to the control over flesh, be it that of people or animals." Indeed, there are countless cases in literature where people get slaughtered as if they were cattle and cows are killed as if they were people. The poet Petronius, for example, relates in his *Satyricon* how during Roman feasts cows were on occasion dressed up as enemy warriors and then dismembered during a kind of symbolic combat, all in plain view of the eaters.

> And with the servants bustling in all directions, a boiled calf was borne in on a silver dish weighing two hundred pounds, and actually wearing a helmet. Then came Ajax, and running like a madman slashed it to bits with his naked sword, and making passes now up and down, collected the pieces on his point and so distributed the flesh among the astonished guests.

In contrast, the soldiers in Bertolt Brecht's *Threepenny Opera* celebrate the killing of their enemies in a song, as if the enemies were cattle. They make, as you might say, "minced meat of them."

> What soldiers live on
> Is heavy cannon,
> From the Cape to Cutch Behar.
> If it should rain one night,
> And they should chance to sight
> Pallid or swarthy faces
> Of uncongenial races
> They'll maybe chop them up to make some
>     beefsteak tatare.

IN REALITY, there's really nothing heroic, let alone predatory, about eating a piece of beef served with herb butter and fries in an Argentine steakhouse. Paradoxically, it is just when *Homo sapiens* wants to act like a bloodthirsty predator that the limitations of the human body become most obvious. Just as humans try to establish their place in primordial nature by eating beef, they're forced to fall back on, of all things, the insignia of (food) culture: they must rely on tools—on knives and forks. A steak knife in this context is more than just a particularly sharp piece of cutlery; it functions, in a sense, as a dental prosthesis, a substitute for the fangs that have shrunk in the course of human evolution.

The only people who are even further removed from the act of killing and carving up cattle than steak eaters are fast-food consumers. They devour cows—hacked into pieces and formed into standardized patties that hardly need

biting or tearing apart—clamped between the two halves of
a bun. Illustrator Gary Larson alludes to that notion in one
of his cartoons. He shows a man pulling a cow out of the
water with his fully bent fishing rod. "Play him, Sidney! Play
him!. . . Oooooooweeeee!" his buddy behind him shouts. "It's
gonna be fresh burgers tonight!" Of course the idea of a cow
behaving like a fish (and being treated like one) is absurdly
funny in itself. The actual joke, however, is that eating a
burger—as opposed to eating a fish you've caught yourself—
just doesn't demand any special skills or physical strength.

More than any other food, the burger epitomizes the spirit
of modern life and is a deeply democratic dish. While having a
piece of meat on the lunch table was the prerogative of the rich
and mighty well into the nineteenth century, innovations in
cattle breeding, transport, and conservation made it increasingly affordable for the lower classes. Minced-meat dishes
had indeed existed since the Middle Ages. The Eurasian Tartar
horse people, for instance, used to eat a raw prototype of the
burger. They allegedly tenderized it by placing it under their
saddles while riding on horseback. But it was in the United
States, the first modern democratic country in the world, that
the *steak tartare*—grilled and shoved into a white bun—first
became a mass-market food. The hamburger probably made
its way to North America with a wave of German immigrants
at the end of the nineteenth century. It first gained nationwide
attention at the World's Fair in St. Louis in 1904. In the spring
of 1955, the first McDonald's restaurant opened in a suburb
of Chicago. The rest is history. Statistically speaking, every
American today eats the meat of seven grown cows in his or
her lifetime, about 40 percent of it in the form of burgers.

The burger accommodates the increasingly mobile and
fast-paced postmodern lifestyle. It's prepared in minutes (or

even just sits under a heat lamp, all garnished and ready to go). It's easy to pack and take away. And if need be, it can be eaten with one hand while the other is on the steering wheel. It's no accident that American fast-food joints got off the ground just as the automobile became a dominant means of mass transport; or that Ray Kroc, the founder of the McDonald's empire, strategically established his first outlets along the roads of the American freeway network. Burgers are therefore fast food in more than one sense. Not only are they served and consumed at an excessive pace; they are often also eaten at great speed. Nothing about a burger is reminiscent of the calm and stolidity of the cow from whose meat it's been made.

Thus the burger represents the endpoint of a long culinary and cultural evolution. In antiquity, and even at the banquets of medieval Europe, animals, as described by Petronius, were mostly served up in their original shape, and only in plain view of the eaters were they cut into pieces. In a burger, however, the cow has been hacked up to such a degree that the meat is hardly recognizable as the muscular tissue of a formerly living being. As Norbert Elias has shown, banishing the carving process to the kitchen backstage is concurrent with the increasing marginalization of death in Western civilization, a development that started at the beginning of the modern era.

At the end of the day, beef in the form of a burger is extremely user-friendly because it is, whether grilled or fried, virtually predigested. In principle even a toddler, though his or her strength might not equal that of the newly born Pantagruel, can eat it without cutlery or much difficulty. In other respects, too, the form in which a burger is served seems ideally suited for children—and for our "childish" contemporary Western society, which wants its physical needs pandered to without fuss or delay. Anyone standing in line at a fast-food chain to order a burger follows his or her pleasure principle in a radical way. Like the breasts of a devoted mother, the desired food is available almost anytime, anywhere. Pedestrian zones, freeway rest areas, and arterial highways are lined with fast-food outlets; once a person reaches the counter, the burger, as McDonald's founder Kroc intended, should take no longer than fifty seconds to be served.

And like the infant, the fast-food customer also knows exactly what to expect. The last thing someone who orders a burger at McDonald's wants is a surprise. A Big Mac tastes pretty much the same from Hamburg to Honolulu. Eating such a burger therefore conveys an odd feeling of familiarity and security. It's even evocative in a way of the act of a mother breastfeeding her infant. "We didn't see the first food we tasted, but we knew it was good and that it came from a beautiful milk vessel, our mother's breast," writes Berlin culinary artist Jochen Fey: "The secret of the fast-food burger's success lies in its packaging, the bun, soft like a mother's breast. Because we eat it with our hands and not with cutlery, it is an unconscious, haptic memory of our first food."

It's revealing that the Golden Arches, the two gracefully curved yellow arcs that form the McDonald's logo, have the shape of plump female breasts. At the same time, they are reminiscent of two semicircular icons, the crescent and the cow horn, both traditional fertility symbols of ancient cattle cults. In a way, the corporation nowadays has taken on the role of a global, divine mother cow that provides her two-legged calves with food. There are, it would seem, understandable motivations for eating burgers, at least until one day you get fed up with eating the same food with the same taste day after day, and, like little Pantagruel, demand "real beef."

# MILK

"COWS," WRITES the philosopher Vilém Flusser, "are efficient machines for turning grass into milk." In 2009 more than 9 million dairy cows grazed in the U.S., altogether yielding more than 21 billion gallons (80 billion liters) of milk. In Canada, during the same period 1.4 million animals produced 2 billion gallons (7.6 billion liters); New Zealand, the world's biggest exporter of milk, supplied over 4 billion gallons (16 billion liters). The average yield of our "milk machines" is about 1,585 gallons (6,000 liters) per annum, with particularly efficient specimens actually producing up to 5,000 gallons (20,000 liters). Compared with that, the contribution of other mammals to our milk supply is negligible.

So when we use the term "milk," we normally mean cow's milk. If we refer to other kinds of milk, we specify their source: mare's milk, goat's milk, breast milk. This usage in itself shows what a special role the cow plays in our perception of mammals: it is the quintessential dairy animal.

Miraculously, our sense of justice and the legal system seem to be in tune in this case: the usage also correlates with a European Union guideline, according to which non-bovine milk has to be labeled as such with an appropriate addendum. Plant-based products, such as the soy-based drink we casually refer to as "soy milk," are denied the precious moniker altogether. As the EU labeling protection act for milk and dairy products unambiguously puts it: "The term 'milk' shall mean exclusively the normal mammary secretion obtained from one or more milkings without either addition thereto or extraction therefrom."

The bureaucratic brevity of this regulation may make the process sound rather simple. It is, however, a complex one. In order to be able to produce milk, a cow must first of all have given birth to a calf. And to fulfill its assigned life task as a dairy cow, it should ideally be pregnant once a year. Nowadays, most cows are mated again as early as six to eight weeks after calving. As soon as the milk forms, the first lactation period—that is, the time during which a cow produces milk—begins. It normally lasts 305 days. After this period, the cow is usually "dried off," meaning that she's not milked, so that the udder can regenerate before the next little calf is born. Then the whole cycle starts all over again, about seven to ten times in a cow's life, though a lot less frequently in high-performance breeds.

The process of milking is no less complicated. In order for the cow to let anyone besides her calf, for whom it was really intended, have her milk, the cow has to be tricked, in a way. The cow that "milks herself" and voluntarily squirts her milk into a hungry human mouth exists only in Indian mythology. To make the cow believe that her suckling calf is

A cow volunteers her milk to the god Venkatesvara.

present, milkers first have to massage the cow's udder. The stimulation causes the cow's pituitary gland to release oxytocin, which causes the milk to be ejected from the glandular tissue of the udder into what's called the cistern, above the teats. The milk is then either milked from the teats by hand, a procedure that, according to expert Michael Brackmann, demands nothing less than the "virtuosity of a violinist." Or the milk is tapped with a milking machine—a lot less virtuosic but gentler on the cow and the milker's hands—the way it has been done since the end of the nineteenth century and as is customary today.

Sometimes, however, these physiological tricks have to be supplemented by psychological manipulation to elicit the much-desired milk from a mother cow. The ancient Egyptians

On the sarcophagus of Queen Kawit, a cow with a calf
tied to her leg bemoans the loss of her milk (2000 BCE).

were already familiar with the technique of tying a cow's calf
to the mother's leg during milking so that the sight and smell
of her own offspring would trigger milk ejection. According
to the Egyptians, this cunning technique not only makes the
milk come down into the udder but also tears come to the
cow's eyes. The mother cow depicted on the sarcophagus of
the priestess Kawit weeps bitterly because she has been bereft
of her milk. In cattle-herding cultures, like that of the Nuer in
East Africa, it's customary to use calf dolls. When a calf dies
in that culture, it's stuffed and placed in front of the cow to
stimulate milk flow.

Besides these kinds of olfactory and optical triggers, audi-
tory stimulus is also used to induce cows to give milk. In his
novel *Tess of the d'Urbervilles*, Thomas Hardy tells of how the
sight of a new milkmaid (Tess, the novel's eponymous her-
oine) makes the cows' milk go "up into their horns." This
metaphor is widely used to describe the fact that cows can

hold back their milk; the psychological and physiological reason for this is usually that the stress hormone adrenaline blocks milk flow. Luckily, the head of the dairy knows what to do:

> "Folks, we must lift up a stave or two—that's the only cure for't." Songs were often resorted to in dairies hereabout as an enticement to the cows when they showed signs of withholding their usual yield; and the band of milkers at this request burst into melody . . . They had gone through fourteen or fifteen verses of a cheerful ballad about a murderer who was afraid to go to bed in the dark because he saw certain brimstone flames around him.

And indeed, as long as the milkers and milkmaids keep on singing, the milk yield shows a "decided improvement." Even today some farmers play music in their sheds to increase their cows' milk production. Unlike the rough Brits of yore, they refrain from using ballads about murderers but usually swear by Mozart, much like parents who believe that the composer's music promotes their newborns' development.

It may seem obvious that the smell and sight of a calf stimulates the cow's pituitary gland or that *Eine kleine Nachtmusik* has a soothing effect that reduces the release of milk-repressing adrenaline. Much more mysterious and controversial in terms of how it works is what is referred to as "cow blowing." In this ritual, air is blown into the cow's vagina or anus—either with a pipe or sometimes directly with the mouth—just prior to milking. The ethnologist Rolf Husmann observed the East African Nuer using this method of cow stimulation and describes it as follows:

The herdsman wipes the cow's vagina with the tas-
sel of her tail. He stands either at her side with his head
tilted sideways or directly behind the cow, embracing
her hind shanks with his hands, and blows air into the
cow's vagina . . . The process is repeated several times.
In between, milking movements are performed on the
teats and the udder is slightly slapped from between the
hind shanks. The Nuer believe that this kind of treatment
encourages the cow to give more milk . . . Once the milking is finished, the youngest herdsman squeezes the last
drops of milk from the teats and licks if off his fingers, or
he may suck it directly from the teats.

The Nuer use this technique mainly for cows that have lost
their calves, but the practice is not restricted to East Africa.
Mahatma Gandhi, for example, writes in his autobiography
that he developed a nauseating aversion to cow's milk and
renounced it when he learned that cows were induced to give
milk by this technique, called phooka in India. When he was
weakened by dysentery, a doctor tried to talk him into drinking milk, but Gandhi steadfastly refused:

> "You can give me the injections," I replied, "but milk is a
> different question; I have a vow against it." "What exactly
> is the nature of your vow?" the doctor inquired. I told
> him the whole history and the reasons behind my vow,
> how, since I had come to know that the cow and buffalo
> were subjected to the process of phooka, I had conceived a
> strong disgust for milk.

In his travelogue "Observations in a Voyage through the
Kingdom of Ireland," written in 1680, Englishman Thomas
Dineley relates that cow blowing was also very common

among Britain's neighbors to the West: "In Milking the Kine when the milk doth not come down freely, they are observ'd in the North of Ireland & elsewhere, either to thrust in a stiff rope or straw of above a foot and a half into the cow's bearing place, or else with their mouths to blow in as much wind as they can, with which doing they many times come off with a shitten nose." Although the actual physiological and psychological benefits of this measure are controversial, its spread across continents and cultures indicates that its benefits outweigh its costs and that it results in a marked increase in milk production—at least according to the herders' subjective view.

CONSIDERING HOW much effort humans go to in wrangling the udder secretions out of a cow, it's hardly surprising that milk has always been highly esteemed as a foodstuff. The German Baroque poet Barthold Heinrich Brockes, for example, interpreted the sight of a herd of cows during milking as nothing less than proof of the existence of God. To him, the mysterious transformation—you could even call it transubstantiation—of grass into milk seemed to clearly indicate the rule of a benign creator:

> Watching you, my dearest cow
> Being milked, I wonder how
> It can be that inside you
> Grass can turn, if all well chewed,
> Into drink as well as food.
> It's a miracle! You do
> Distill goodness all for free.
> Tell me, human, that indeed
> To him who all this has decreed
> Now and always glory be!

In vegetarian cultures—in India, for example—where milk is an important source of animal protein, innumerable expressions and metaphors attest to the great value attributed to milk and dairy products. Modern Tamil describes having pleasant thoughts as drinking "the milk of the mind." Similarly, the feeling of compassion is likened to the sensation of milk collecting in the breast, and the effect that friendly words have on the human soul to milk being poured into the stomach. Among the Indian Coorg, forgoing all pleasure while mourning the dead is seen as an expression of piety—and that means, most of all, not drinking milk during that period. And so one of the worst insults one Coorg can hurl at another Coorg is, "I will drink milk when you die!"

ONE QUALITY that has been attributed to milk is its ability to imbue those who drink it with a special strength. From a scientific point of view, it's largely true that milk is healthy. Research shows that drinking milk can prevent medical conditions such as osteoporosis, high blood pressure, and obesity and that the calcium in milk is important for healthy bones. Beyond that, the belief that milk gives you strength is also a kind of symbolic transference. In the same way that ritual cannibalism is about incorporating another human's strength by eating certain parts of his or her body and in the same way that meat eaters supposedly assimilate the strength of cattle when they eat a bloody steak, we secretly hope that drinking milk will make us as strong as fully grown cows.

This explains why cows, when they make an appearance in milk ads, are often portrayed as especially strong animals (which is quite ironic considering that cows on most commercial farms don't drink milk but are fed artificial milk formula from an early age). For years now, the commercials and ads of the Swiss Milk Producers' Association, for example, have featured a cow named Lovely, showing her in always novel and extreme situations of great absurdity. Sometimes she wears a huge bell, its size more appropriate for a belfry, around her strong neck. Sometimes she appears as a karate cow, smashing two stacked-up concrete slabs into bits with her front hooves. At other times, Lovely successfully fights against a sumo wrestler, a boxing kangaroo, and a rhinoceros, whose broken-off horn lies pathetically on the ground after the fight. A commercial for the German company Müller Milk sends a similar message. Here, a cow scores a sporting success in a horse derby. At first it seems as if the usual thoroughbreds with names like Lucky Star and Freedom are going to win the race. But then the commentator's voice erupts with excitement: "And Elsa comes from behind!" A cow comes galloping past the field, confidently takes the lead, and, cheered on by the spectators, finishes first. A close-up of the cow's billowing udder leaves no doubt about the secret of Elsa's strength. At the end of the commercial, during the victory ceremony, an announcement divulges what will happen to the contents of the udder: "Only the milk of the best cows goes into Müller Milk." Strong cows, the underlying message implies, give strong milk, and those who drink it can partake in this strength. There's something rather comical about the fact that in the commercial Elsa behaves totally un-cow-like and acts like, of all things, her traditional archenemy, the horse.

In the movie *Kung Pow: Enter the Fist*, we encounter a similarly tragicomic cow. A karate match between the movie's hero, the "Chosen One," and his evil adversary's martial-arts-trained cow is undisputedly the climax of this martial arts parody. For several minutes, the skills of the two fighters are evenly balanced. But then the Chosen One uses a perfidious trick and manages to turn the tables in his favor: he throws himself under the cow's belly, grabs her udder with both hands, and simply milks the cow empty. Deprived of her milk and thus her strength, the computer-animated cow collapses. Her opponent leaves the scene victorious. However much the movie scene and the Müller Milk commercial may vary in their style and intended effect, they do have one thing in common: they suggest that those who have milk in their bodies, be it in an udder or in the digestive tract, have superhuman strength.

Likewise, a recent campaign by the California Milk Processor Board ("Got milk?") suggested, if facetiously, that milk can give humans extraordinary powers. The campaign is centered on a fictitious eccentric glam-rock star named White Gold, whose only form of nourishment is milk. He even plays a transparent guitar filled with the "white gold," enabling him to improvise and imbibe at the same time. This habit, or so the campaign claims, is what has turned White Gold from a wreck on skid row into a healthy, sexy, muscular rock star. "Before the luscious white mane, the four-hour guitar solos and ripped abdominals, there was White Gold, the man. A mess of frail hair, a dull smile, and a scrawny body . . . Then something changed. White Gold's voice started sounding like nothing ever heard before . . . His sculpted biceps were shredding his T-shirts. His skin had a sexy, healthy glow. Gossip columns questioned whether White Gold had work done. He strongly denied it, saying, 'Everyone needs to chill, like my milk does. It's all good. I'm just a vessel for the white genius to flow.'"

BUT MILK doesn't just make you strong; it also makes you gentle and peaceful (karate cows are a rare exception to this rule). When Shakespeare's bloodthirsty Lady Macbeth bemoans her husband's hesitation to kill the King without further ado, she attributes it to his mind's being "too full of the milk of human kindness." In Zimbabwe, when someone is said to be possessed by the devil, a priest will sometimes pour milk over him to purify his soul. The underlying idea is that by drinking milk, we become as calm and relaxed as a ruminating cow. Drinking the traditional glass of milk before going to bed is a symbol of this kind of magical thinking.

The idea is rooted not only in the enviable calm that cows exude but also in our own growth and development. Milk, in the form of breast milk, is usually the first food we ingest, and it's the only complete, stand-alone form of nourishment. When we are breastfed, we find ourselves in a state of archetypal unity with our mother's body, a state that the French psychoanalyst Jacques Lacan termed *jouissance*. We lack nothing; we desire nothing—apart from more milk, maybe. As soon as the newborn feels its mother's breast between its lips and the white secretion running down its throat, it is in "heaven." Even the Promised Land in the Bible is referred to as the "land flowing with milk and honey."

When the infant is weaned, this heavenly unity is, however, destroyed, and with that the time of innocence ends. As soon as our mother stops breastfeeding us, we are forced to resort to other kinds of food. We wrest the seeds and roots away from plants, we pinch the unborn offspring of chickens the minute they are laid, we take the lives of fish and mammals, and, while the latter are still alive, we take away their milk. Only by drinking it can we fool ourselves into thinking that we can, at least for a moment, return to a state of primordial innocence.

Photographer Annie Leibovitz's photo of Whoopi Goldberg bathing very vividly illustrates the return to a paradise lost. We see the actress from a bird's-eye perspective lying in a freestanding enamel bathtub. Her thighs are apart, her bent legs held upwards, her arms stretched out over her head. She lies spread-eagled like a baby whose diapers are being changed; her face is distorted into a rapt grimace. Whoopi Goldberg is lying in a bathtub full of milk. If she were to slide down another inch, the lake of milk would pour into her open mouth; another hand's breadth and the actress would sink into it completely. If she drowns in it, she will once again be completely at one with herself.

Although childlike and unselfconscious, the photo is also rather erotic—Goldberg's body posture, her ecstatic facial expression and, most of all, the milk that surrounds her hint that a sexual act has recently taken place. The partner, although invisible or just gone, has left enormous amounts of his semen in the bathtub.

The similarities between milk and semen and, in parallel to that, between a cow's teats and a man's penis, can't be overlooked. It's quite striking that the act of milking, during which an opaque white viscous jet spurts out of an elongated organ that has been tenderly massaged is reminiscent of male masturbation. "So we see that this . . . fantasy of sucking a penis has the most innocent origin," writes Sigmund Freud. "It is a recasting of what may be described as a prehistoric impression of sucking at the mother's or nurse's breast. . . In most instances, a cow's udder has aptly played the part of an image intermediate between a nipple and a penis." The

German musician and writer Heinz Strunk therefore always uses the term "milking the lizard" when referring to the act of masturbation in his book *Fleisch ist mein Gemüse* (Meat is my vegetable). And authors Dieter Schnack and Rainer Neutzling report of a woman who claims to have perceived conception as "being fed," and her husband's semen "as breast milk." Because of that, she allegedly felt "like a well-fed baby" during the first few weeks of her pregnancy. Accordingly, sucking a mother's breast and, even more so, the (rather less frequently practiced) act of drinking directly from a cow's udder are reminiscent of the act of fellatio.

So milk is said to have a variety of very special qualities. It allegedly makes us strong and helps improve bone strength. It makes us peaceable and calm and reminds us of the time when we were infants and of a lost paradise. It's the epitome of all things nutritious and fertile. As such it has female and, to a lesser degree, male connotations. Because of its opaque— well, milky—consistency, it's also quite mysterious. We can, literally, not see through it. But most of all, it's white.

Just how important this color is to the way we perceive milk as a healthy and morally and hygienically "pure" substance is easy to appreciate in situations where it's not white. The most famous example is probably the metaphor with which the poet Paul Celan starts his poem "Death Fugue": "Black milk of daybreak, we drink it in the evening / we drink it at noon and in the morning / we drink it at night / we drink and we drink." The historical background to this poem is the Shoah, the systematic mass murder of European Jews during the Third Reich. The crime marked a radical fracture of civilization, a breach that, to this day, calls into question the very foundations of Western morality and culture. In the poem, this complete reversal of all values is succinctly and disquietingly mirrored by the image of black milk.

Whether the milk that Celan describes just *looks* black in the darkness of the early morning hours or whether it *is* indeed black is of minor importance. What is crucial is that the contradiction in terms of the phrase and the negative adjective calls into question everything that milk symbolizes—vitality, placidity, motherly care, "human kindness," and the Promised Land that flows with milk and honey— and turns it into its opposite. If something white suddenly looks black, then there is war instead of peace; motherly and human love turn into hate; and even the most livable country is transformed into a place from which we'd best flee as soon as possible. In view of such a fundamentally corrupted world order, the only hope for improved circumstances exists *ex negativo*—that is, in the imagination of all that currently doesn't exist.

However closely the black milk metaphor is linked with the name Paul Celan in our collective memory, he was not the first one to use it in poetry. In her poem "Into Life," the poetess Rose Ausländer, who like Celan came from Czernowitz, had already talked about "black milk and heavy absinth" that sprang from the "motherly intimacy" of grief. It seems black milk here has a function similar to black gall, the bodily fluid that, according to ancient humorism, was responsible for melancholy.

Discolored milk is also a source of melancholy in a song by blues singer Robert Johnson (who, in contrast to Paul Celan, certainly was not influenced by Rose Ausländer). In his piece "Milkcow's Calf Blues," recorded in 1937, he accuses a cow:

Tell me, milk cow, what on earth is wrong with you?
Ooh, milk cow, what on earth is wrong with you?
Now you have a little new calf, ooh, and your milk
     is turnin' blue.

Your calf is hungry, I believe he needs a suck,
Your calf is hungry, ooh, I believe he needs a suck,
But your milk is turnin' blue, ooh, I believe he's outta luck.

The blue milk of the mother cow appears to be a metaphor for the singer's blues. It remains unknown why exactly the milk is discolored, but the reasons for the blues quickly become clear: the cow is behaving like an unreliable lover. The calf, which is hungry and needs feeding urgently, is a symbol for the singer himself. And the blame for the discord between cow and calf lies, as is so often the case, with another man, or, to stick with the metaphor, another bull.

My milk cow's been ramblin', ooh, for miles around,
My milk cow's been ramblin', ooh, for miles around,
Well, now she been troublin' some other bull cow, ooh,
     Lord, in this man's town.

So the cow has been unfaithful. She has thrown herself at another fleshy bull and made the cuckold singer "wear horns," an offense which in the macho blues universe has been known to be punished by instant execution. We can only hope that the "milk cow" fares better than the protagonist of Norbert Kaser's prose poem "a cow." Unlike Robert Johnson's unfaithful animal, Kaser's cow may not have "brought . . . anyone misfortune," but she still has to die for the simple reason that her milk has a blue tinge:

she gave ample milk without kicking during milking and
without refusing her milk only its milk had a bluish tinge
(like in the alpine dairy) . . . but blue isn't good say the
farmers the cow is bewitched. so they decide to slaughter the harbinger of misfortune during the night . . . the
corpse was laboriously buried in the dunghill by candle-
light lanterns & newfangled batteries. the next day roses
flowered on the "grave."

In fact, in the old days, milk with a blue discoloration, as Johnson and Kaser described, seems to have occurred frequently.
It was, however, not due to unfaithful or bewitched dairy
cows. According to biologist Herbert Seiler, it's the result of
the milk's being contaminated with a variant of the bacterium
*Pseudomonas fluorescens*—which goes to show that milk shares
yet another characteristic with love: it can go sour very quickly.

# HIDE AND HAIR

THE DEVIL has a vested interest in making sure that none of our misdeeds are overlooked after we die and that as many souls as possible join him in hell. Which is why, according to medieval beliefs, he records our sins with painstaking accuracy. To do that, he uses parchment made from the skins of sheep or calves. If he wants to document an especially large number of sins, he needs a larger sheet—one made from the hide of a fully grown cow. And if one individual has committed so many sins that they exceed even the scope deemed reasonable by the devil, then even the largest possible parchment size won't suffice to do the bookkeeping. In that case, the German language describes the sins, follies, and failures of the damned person as "impossible to fit onto a cowhide."

There are, of course, tricks to enlarge the surface of a cowhide. The mythical Queen Dido, for instance, is said to have fled her native Phoenicia, ending up in the region of today's Tunis with a handful of loyalists. Not really well-disposed toward the newcomers, the ruling King Iarbas sold the queen only the amount of land that could be covered with the hide of a cow. The cunning Dido just cut the leather into thin strips and used it to fence in a large piece of land with a view of the ocean, enabling her to purchase a property big enough for a citadel at a bargain price. Supposedly that's why the hill above the harbor of Carthage is to this day called *byrsa*, or "the cowhide."

As these examples show, cowhides are very versatile. Once a cow has been skinned, the hide is preserved through tanning with chemicals. As such, it's an important base material for shoes, jackets, belts, saddles, sofas, sandals, transmission belts, tepees, exercise balls, S&M costumes, and fine bindings of books. The hair that grows on the hide helps humans to differentiate the various cow races and, if it has the right color, it's used as an advertising medium. Nowadays, the black-and-white coat pattern of the Holstein is the sign of cowness. The cowhide has literally become detached from the cow. It almost seems as if it has crossed the limits of practical use to become a kind of screen onto which we can project new images of the cow.

BARTHOLD HEINRICH BROCKES saw the cowhide mostly as an object of aesthetic pleasure. The poem "Die Heerde Kühe" (The herd of cows) is featured in his collection *Irdisches Vergnügen in Gott* (Earthly joy in God). Brockes's nature poems reflect his close observations of the natural world. They attempt to paint the picture of a benign creator who reveals himself to the world in an approachable as well as visually pleasing way. In the case of the herd described in his poem, this earthly joy arises not only from the fact that cows can turn grass into milk but also that they display a great variety of coats:

The different colors bring a smile onto my face.
How lovely, pleasant, full of grace,
To see that some
Are smoothly black and others glowing red.
Bluish-gray skins adorn
Some pretty cows, and they in turn the meadow's spread.
With grace and pride the coats are worn
Where spots of red and flecks of black
The white sides, bathed in light,
With a variety of shapes bedeck.
Those with a curly coat shine from afar so bright.
The forefront's white in most, untarnished,
In high-gloss black their muzzles shine
As if on purpose varnished
With body-paint of most divine design,
So pleasant to the eye.

We don't know which pasture the poet was standing in when he wrote this ode to cows. Did he really see such great variety of differently colored coats—black, red, bluish-gray ones—in a single herd? Or did he take a certain poetic license and just cram various cows that he had seen on other occasions onto a single fictitious pasture for the sake of this poem? Nowadays such a sight would be rather unusual. Most cow herds are made up of members of a single breed.

However, in northern Germany, where Brockes lived and worked, systematic cattle breeding had not yet been introduced during the poet's lifetime. The coat of the local Black-and-White breed therefore was not necessarily black-and-white but had a variety of colors. It was only at the end of the eighteenth century that it became important in the North

German marshes that the coats of local cows all be pure white with a black pattern. The reasons for that shift were partially economic. Lured by the legendary milk production of the Black-and-Whites, more and more buyers from other regions in Germany came to purchase a specimen for their own sheds. With blood tests and genetic analysis not yet available to determine lineage, coat color and pattern were the most important indicators of the cattle's origins. Rumor has it that cows were therefore often enhanced with color, scissors, or bleach in order to achieve the desired coat pattern.

So back then, coat color served not only to delight the eye or to prove that there is a benign God. It also functioned as an identifier: it showed to which general or regional breed a cow belonged. A passage from Arnold Stadler's novel *Mein Hund, meine Sau, mein Leben* (My dog, my hog, my life) illustrates how closely the coat of a cow was associated with the animal's regional origin. The Swabian writer describes the conflicts that arise in a small village community in rural Southern Germany, when a herd of cows "immigrates"—or to be more precise, is imported by rail—from the both geographically and culturally distant marshes of Frisia in Northern Germany.

> Ideological questions needed to be addressed. Black cows! The black cow! Because the fact that there were black cows in our shed, delivered from Leer in East Frisia to the train station in Mindersdorf, was, in the eyes of the Schwackenreuthers, treason against the famous brown Meßkirch Highland Fleckvieh, an apostasy from the true faith . . . Uncle Cider shouted into the room that the (brown) Meßkirch Highland Fleckvieh cow was a real cow . . . The black cow, infiltrated from the north,

threatened to destroy his native land—nay, his existence. This foreign apparition (from Northern Germany) would not eat his native grass. And that's what all of Schwackenreuthe thought . . . After all, the area wasn't called Fleckvieh county for nothing.

There is no sign here of Brockes's delight in the variety of colors. It has been replaced by a fear that the local cattle stock might be swamped with "foreign" cows. It would seem that the resident brown Highland Fleckvieh determines the region's identity, even gives it its name. The "black cow," by contrast, signifies a hard-to-identify alien threat, the unknown—nay, the scary: Northern Germany; immigration; globalization, which has arrived in Schwackenreuthe, even if it's in the shape of a differently colored cow. For the narrow-minded locals and their traditional cattle, the black cow's arrival is the epitome of the worst-case scenario.

The diabolical black cow threatens the very foundations of the identity of the Fleckvieh county inhabitants. So much so that Uncle Cider's claim—based solely on the color of her coat—that she isn't a "real cow" at all is met with no opposition whatsoever. The discussion surrounding color corresponds to the traditional Eurocentric discourse on human "race." Since the seventeenth century, skin color had been considered the most important distinguishing feature of various ethnicities. Here too, a "standard" color defined humanity. And the relatively light tone of one's own skin was naturally assumed to be the basic anthropological color, while "black" signified radical otherness, the inhuman, and therefore either the devil or the inhabitants of other continents. Although this view has thankfully changed—for one thing, we now know that the first humans lived in Africa and that the "standard color" of humankind must therefore have been considerably darker than that of "white" Europeans—it still appears to survive in certain circles, if only applied to cows.

A COMMERCIAL that was broadcast in Italy in 2001, five years after Stadler's novel was first published, uses the same kind of subliminal fear. The ad shows a herd of black-and-white cows peacefully grazing in a pasture. A fence protects them from the outside world; no evil seems to threaten the unsuspecting animals. But adversity on four legs is in the offing. A brown-patched cow, apparently not part of the herd and therefore not allowed into the fenced-off area, strolls along the wooden enclosure in a conspicuously inconspicuous manner. She glances around furtively. She ignores a sign that identifies the bucolic landscape beyond it as *Zona di Produzione Parmigiano Reggiano* and with surprising elegance jumps sideways over the fence. A local cowherd manages to immediately ward her off the pasture, but not for long. The Red-and-White just keeps on trying. During her next attempt, she digs a tunnel under the fence with her hooves, like a fugitive trying to get across a tightly patrolled border. The forbidden garden with the black-and-white cows seems to hold a special attraction for the foreign cow.

The commercial is obviously not about the defense of a particularly lush pasture but about the protection of an extremely lucrative market segment. The film was commissioned by a consortium of northern Italian cheese makers. They were no longer willing to put up with the fact that hard cheeses from other regions or countries were sold under names like parmesan, *Parmezano* or other misleading designations that sounded similar to *Parmigiano*. In their opinion, only hard cheese produced in the region around Parma should be allowed to be labeled *Parmigiano*. A 1996 verdict by the European Court proved them right and gave non-Parma hard cheese producers five years to come up with new names for their products. Most of them let the deadline pass without taking any action.

What's interesting about this commercial is that a regional designation is linked with a certain coat color and thus to a certain breed of cow. In reality a variety of breeds graze in the area around Parma: brown cows, Red-and-Whites, Holsteins, as well as the famous *Vacche Rosse*, the traditional rose-colored cows of the Apennine Peninsula. They all give milk from which *Parmigiano* is made. The most crucial factor for being allowed to use the cheese makers consortium's quality label is that the cows get enough fresh fodder. Careful production and a long aging process are also important.

By identifying the strictly controlled *Zona di Produzione Parmigiano Reggiano* with cows of a single coat color, the commercial seems to suggest that only a certain breed is entitled to live and "work" there. This (consciously or unconsciously) evokes connotations of other illegal border crossings, like the ones that were taking place with increasing frequency about 620 miles (1,000 kilometers) farther south, in the Strait of Messina at the time. It was through this narrow passage between the island of Sicily and mainland Italy that refugees attempted to get from North Africa to the European mainland by boat. Since Italy is geographically closest among the EU countries to the African continent, this is where most of these refugees tend to arrive. It's no coincidence that the commercial is entitled *L'Intrusa*, the intruder. In 2004, when the suffering of refugees on the southern coast of Italy hit the headlines of German newspapers, the commercial was finally replaced by a different, funnier one. Rather than digging tunnels or engaging in other politically suspicious activities, the cow with the colored coat has a go at pole vaulting.

IT'S SOMEWHAT ironic that the breed featured as the rightful inhabitant of the Parma region in L'Intrusa is one that certainly wouldn't be found there: the black-and-white Holstein. Neither the strict cowherd in the commercial nor Arnold Stadler's Uncle Cider could have prevented the worldwide spread of the *Holsteinisch-Friesische* breed, which settlers from northern Germany introduced to North America in the seventeenth century. From there it spread throughout the world under its American name Holstein-Friesian or Holstein for short. In Germany, half of all dairy cows today are Holsteins, and not just the ones from the regions of Holstein or Friesland.

Farmers appreciate the Holstein because of her phenomenal milk yield. One reason the breed is also popular with nonfarmers and advertising executives is her prevalence. Perfunctory observers of cows will probably be most familiar with the sight of a Holstein. Then again, her distinctive coat pattern also contributes to her popularity. Just like black-and-brown rosettes on a yellow coat epitomize leopards and longitudinal black-and-white stripes zebras, black patches on a white background unambiguously signify *cow*. In terms of color, the warm, golden coat of the Jersey cow or the fiery red ones of Scottish Highland cattle are no less attractive. But detached from the cow's body, they are hardly recognizable as bovine body hair.

The fact that we have in a way chosen the cow's appearance—that is, the color of her coat—to define the essence of her nature shows just how superficial our understanding of the animal is. Even the most un-cow-like items—teacups, backpacks, bed linen, or a computer mouse—can now be "cowified" with the black-and-white pattern of the Holstein and marketed as a witty cow accessory. With this color pattern, even totally unrelated animals can achieve the status of cow family members. In 2001, the German dairy company Müller ran an ad campaign in Italy. A majestic lion stared down from large billboards. In contrast to his fellow lions, he wasn't sporting a yellow coat but the black-and-white one of a Holstein. The caption next to his white-haired head identified him not as the ruler of the animal kingdom but as *Re Latte*: "The king of milk."

MUCH AS the cow is stripped of her hide only for it to be put on other animals or all kinds of objects, the cow's body is covered with ever new surfaces and signs—she constantly gets reclothed in new skin. In this respect, the TV station RTL, normally not known for subtlety, acted with relative delicacy. In 2007, to advertise its docusoap "Farmer Seeks Wife," in which single farmers are hooked up with other singles, it published a postcard on which a black-and-white cow looked at the viewer with big, trusting eyes. Only upon careful inspection did one realize that there was something wrong with the patches on her flanks: they were all heart shaped. There was even an amorous little red heart, which, unlike the black patches, had ostensibly been added by a farmer who had gotten lucky in love.

The most adulterated cow hide, as far as color is concerned, is undoubtedly the one sported by the cow advertising Milka brand chocolate. As a symbol for the milk that the chocolate contains, as well as for the Suchard company's home country of Switzerland, she has been featured on the brand's packaging since 1901. In keeping with the color preferences of the Art Nouveau era, the first paper wrappers on the "melt-in-your-mouth seductive" chocolate were entirely purple: the cow, the farmer who accompanied her, the mountains. Only during the twentieth century did the landscape regain its natural color. The purple color eventually stuck only to the cow's hide and became the brand's unique selling proposition. In photos the color effect was achieved by touching up an original image. Commercials, in contrast, involved a two-hour process during which the cow's coat was painstakingly hand painted.

In 1992 alone, twenty different cows had to endure this make-up procedure. All of them were Simmental cows, a breed that had impressed the art director in charge of the advertising campaign with its rich patch variety. Across Europe, the image of the Milka cow has become standardized: a Simmental from the left, her head slightly inclined, with precisely defined lettering and patches. The distinctive purple tone of her hide became a Europe-wide registered color trademark in 1995. According to a survey conducted in German preschools in the early nineties, more than half of the children believed that cows are purple. The Suchard company—now part of Kraft Foods—has made its mark on the cow. In the past, cows were branded with a glowing iron; today it suffices to digitally enhance the cow's appearance in advertising, the corporate communications method of "branding."

An extension of this idea is to put the hide of another animal on a cow. The Dutch painter and writer Jan Cremer, for instance, in his 1973 lithography *Dutch Heritage (from Indonesia)* crossed a local cow with a tiger. The cow is standing in

Jan Cremer's *Dutch Heritage (from Indonesia)* (1973). © Jan Cremer/SODRAC (2001).

a field of tulips under a red sun. Her body is depicted in profile. She has her head turned toward the viewer and looks at the viewer perplexedly, as if she isn't too sure herself what exactly happened to her. Her coat features the characteristic yellow and black markings of a large Indonesian wildcat. Her raised tail, which gives an ostentatious, uninhibited view of her vulva, is also more reminiscent of a tiger than a cow.

At first sight, the picture seems to be making fun of the cow. The shrill, menacing predator guise really highlights the cow's domesticated, somewhat obsequious character. She almost looks a bit like a dutiful bank teller who's suddenly decided to wear Native American war paint. At the same time, the picture can also be interpreted as a nasty commentary on Dutch demographics. For almost 350 years, the Indonesian archipelago was under Dutch rule, and the island kingdom was a colony until 1949. Consequently, many people of Indonesian origin live in the country of their colonial rulers today and constitute the largest ethnic minority in the Netherlands. By indicating through the title of his picture that the depicted animal is a "cow of Dutch extraction," by adding the ironically qualifying parenthesis that she comes "from Indonesia," and by presenting such a strange mongrel creation, Jan Cremer delivers a subliminal message: this is an unnatural hybrid. The "real" Dutch, be they cows or humans, look different.

In 2001, the Swiss clothing company Tarzan produced an advertising postcard that followed a similar aesthetic principle, albeit without the politically questionable overtones. In that picture, too, a real local cow was shown in a real local landscape. And this cow, too, had been adulterated: she was wearing a leopard hide, modeled on the loincloth of the yodeling jungle hero. The geographic origin of the donor animal was presumably irrelevant; the point was that the cow had finally dared to wear something other than the boring old cowhide.

At around the same time that the leopard cow appeared in Basel county, the principle "old cow, new hide" reached the apex of its popularity, essentially as a result of the so-called CowParades. At these events, life-size fiberglass cows, paid for by sponsors, are painted by artists, exhibited in pedestrian zones or shopping malls and then auctioned off for charity. The first parade of this kind took place in Switzerland in 1998, then still under the motto "Zurich Cow Culture." The concept proved incredibly popular and gave rise to an almost epidemic propagation of fiberglass animals at the beginning of the new millennium. Soon every European and North American city seemed to hold a CowParade. Nowadays the idea is being marketed internationally and exported to all continents.

A leopard cow on an ad for Swiss clothing company Tarzan.

According to the American CowParade Holdings Corporation the global CowParades are "the world's largest public art
event." Such an interpretation presumes a rather broad concept of art. Quite frequently the psychedelic patterns, Matisse
imitations, and local cityscapes that are painted onto the
cows, as well as the titles that go with them ("Cower Bridge,
London") seem more like an extension of sidewalk art on a
different medium. The exhibition organizers may well pre-
tend to be interested in the cow as an "art object," but for
most artists the hide of the artificial cows is really more of a
strangely convex canvas for their often very pleasing pictures.

So it's hardly surprising that one of the few renowned
and really innovative artists invited to take part in the Cow-
Parade was immediately disinvited when he submitted his
draft. When working on the subject for the 2000 CowParade in New York, filmmaker and painter David Lynch didn't
restrict himself to just changing the surface of his fiberglass
cow but penetrated deep into her insides. Lynch chopped off
the cow's head, placed it on her back, on which he had previ-
ously inflicted a deep wound, and rammed a fistful of knives

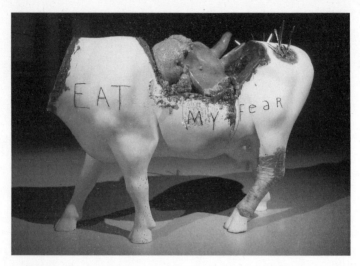

David Lynch's *Eat My Fear*, banned from the New York CowParade in 2000.

and forks into the cow's flesh. He then poured red paint over her head and wounds and wrote the sentence "EAT MY FEAR" onto her flanks. The representative of New York City Hall who was in charge of the event execution went on record as saying that the sight of Lynch's cow reminded him of Charles Manson—who in 1969 incited his Manson Family members to commit several brutal murders and claimed to be Satan himself.

All of this brings us back to the devil and the burning question of how many sins, misdeeds, and follies you have to commit in order to wear out the patience and the recording system of old Beelzebub and make sure you end up in hell for sure. When is the devil's parchment completely covered with entries? How much fits onto a cowhide? The coat of a fully grown cow measures approximately 55 square feet (5 square meters), equivalent to the surface of a bit less than

95 letter-size (or 90 A4-size) sheets of paper. Working on the assumption that the devil, too, has to save paper and is using both sides of his parchments, he has roughly 200 pages at his disposal. Since about 1,500 characters fit onto a standard page, the catalogue of sins is definitely full when we reach 270,000 characters. For comparison, this volume contains about 340,000 characters—which goes to show that not even a book about cows fits onto a cowhide.

# UDDER AND VULVA

OF ALL animals that are bred for dairy production, the cow
has by far the biggest and most distinctive udder. It dangles between her hind legs, heavy and swollen, as soon
as the cow gives birth to her first calf at the age of about two.
From then on, some high-yield breeds like the Holstein can
produce more than 25 gallons (100 liters) of milk a day—at
least immediately after giving birth, in the first phase of the
cow's lactation period.

Partly because of its remarkable size, and possibly also
partly because of its shape and its color, which resembles
human skin (at least that of most Central Europeans), the
udder of the cow is often compared to the female breast. The
fact that cows have only one set of mammary glands but four
teats seems to be of minor significance.

The comparison works the other way as well. According
to this sexist school of thought women don't just have udders
like cows—cows also have a sort of breast between their legs.
The cover of Aerosmith's 1993 album *Get a Grip* is adorned

with a close-up of a cow udder, a visual complement to the title's double entendre. Only a minor detail points to the fact that the organ to be groped is not a "regular" udder. The front right teat of the four-legged rocker girl—a black-and-white Holstein like the one featured on the cover of Pink Floyd's album *Atom Heart Mother* twenty years earlier—sports a piercing akin to a nipple ring.

In a similar fashion, a friendly, light-brown cow faced the visitors of the 2001 Zurich Street Parade (a forerunner of the San Francisco LoveFest and much like the New Orleans Mardi Gras celebrations). Poised above the tagline "Milk. The pick-me-up of the Zurich Strip Parade," she looked at partygoers from posters and half-page newspaper ads. She licked her parted lips lasciviously like a bovine Bettie Page, swung her tail seductively, and was dressed in nothing but a shiny, rainbow-colored lace bra, which enveloped her udder and was attached by a fancy gold chain slung across her back.

Firstly, it's remarkable that the ad's designers didn't choose a traditional Swiss cow as their model but rather a modern hybrid of Simmental and Brown Swiss, a very productive milk-producing breed with a very pronounced udder. It's also noteworthy that the cow wears a bra, which ironically makes the covered (and soon to be revealed) body part more erotic and desirable than it otherwise would have been. In other words, the bra strips the cow.

One thing is certain: the cow's udder is not just an organ that produces and distributes milk but also one that is perceived as a symbol of sexual excitability and attractiveness. It's no coincidence that the comic book character Clarabelle Cow, who in earlier Walt Disney films and comic strips appeared with a bare udder, was from 1931 onward shown fully clothed.

As *Time Magazine* reported, various censor boards had been upset by the "gargantuan organ" of the cow, "whose antics of late have shocked some and convulsed others." The cow is ultimately not just a nurturer and mother but also a *woman*.

The most extreme expression of "animal love" for cows is what is referred to as zoophilia, the sexual relationship between humans and animals. It has for centuries been an important taboo subject, especially in the homeland of the Zurich Street Parade. One chapter in the famous sexologist Magnus Hirschfeld's 1930 book *Geschlecht und Verbrechen* (Sexuality and crime) is titled "Sodomy in Switzerland." In it he describes how as early as in the fifteenth century the Swiss already "had an international reputation for having sexual relationships with cattle in particular. Although almost fanatically and bigotedly pious at the time, they still seemed to provide more than ample ammunition for this accusation."

Hirschfeld's deduction, arguably somewhat tenuous, that sexual encounters with cows were commonplace in Switzerland at the time, is based on the fact that the Swiss showed an especially sensitive reaction to all expressions having to do with cows—evidence, Hirschfeld felt, that a guilty conscience needs no accuser. "They reacted so badly to expletives involving cows," he writes, "that offenders were sentenced to capital punishment, even if the expressions were not used as direct accusations but just as swearwords." The Swiss expression *Kühgyer* or *Kue-Gehijer* for a man who *gehijet*—"penetrates"— cows was perceived as particularly insulting, and therefore those who used it were regularly punished with death. In 1470, for example, a foreigner was sentenced to death by drowning, because he (presumably mockingly) had remarked that "*die eidgenossenschaft sey ein guet frey land und ob einer eine kuh*

**Ein Warhafftig vnd Erschröcklich**
Gepurt eines Kalbs welches von einer Kue gebo-
ren ist worden den xviiij tag Hewmon des
Sechsvndfunfftzigsten Jars.

A pamphlet from 1556 illustrating the perils of sexual
relations with cows: a ghastly man-cow bastard.

*gehye . . . so tüege man ihm nüt darumb"*—in English: "Switzerland is a free country, and if someone abuses a cow there, he
won't be punished."

This claim had grave consequences for the cheeky non-
Swiss, and it was also factually wrong: not only could the
verbal abuse of Swiss citizens as cow lovers be penalized with
a death sentence but also the act of *Kühgyen* itself. During the
Middle Ages, bestiality carried the death penalty in the entire
Christian-influenced West. This was in accordance with a
stipulation of the Old Testament: "If there is a man who lies
with an animal, he should surely be put to death; you shall
also kill the animal . . . They shall surely be put to death;
their bloodguiltiness is upon them." Even the oldest codex
of the Hittites, which may have influenced the genesis of the

Hebrew code of law, demanded that "if a man lies with a cow, the punishment is death."

One important reason for this prohibition was perhaps the belief that such an illegal alliance could produce a bastard child, a monster, that would torment humans in the name of God if they didn't atone for this kind of lapse. Numerous pamphlets from the early modern period illustrate the possible consequences of cross-breeding humans and animals. One of them is a pamphlet from 1556 that highlights the "really horrific birth of a calf born of a cow": "This calf has four calf legs and a big human head, a black beard, two tiny human ears, a man's chest and back . . . and the calf did not live long."

In Switzerland, breaches of the bestiality law were mercilessly prosecuted up until the eighteenth century. In 1605, after having been tortured, a herdsman from Erschwil, for example, was sentenced to death by burning at the stake for "having twice committed un-Christian deeds with the miller's cow he was minding." In 1660, the night watchman of the small town of Liestal was beheaded and burned after returning home one May night with "soiled trousers," which was taken as evidence that he had had sexual intercourse with a cow. And in 1756, a peasant boy from Zeglingen was sentenced to lifelong service on a galley after having been to a cow shed. He only escaped death because it was established that once he had climbed onto the milking stool behind the "little cow" it "wouldn't stay still," thus keeping him from "executing this atrocity."

Magnus Hirschfeld was able to prove that between 1400 and 1800 sodomy with cows constituted a third of all sex offenses punished with the death sentence in Zurich. In Lucerne, the same offense accounted for as much as half of all capital punishment cases between 1500 and 1800. Hirschfeld concluded from this that sex with cows in Switzerland was the "most widespread sex offense," presumably because in the case of Swiss tillers and Alpine cowherds, "the nature of their activities . . . possibly exposed them more to sexual intercourse with cows than [those in] other countries." The sexual offender was usually burned; the chronicles Hirschfeld examined didn't comment on whether, in accordance with the Old Testament, the cows were always burned as well. It seems the offense occurred so frequently that the court reporters hardly ever noted down the exact details of the punishment. But Hirschfeld speculates that the cows were occasionally spared for economic reasons.

ZOOPHILIA IS of course not just a phenomenon of dark times long past. According to a study by American biology professor Alfred Kinsey, 8 percent of all men (and 3.5 percent of women) in the U.S. have sexual contact with animals. European research points to a figure of about 5 percent of the total population, with the number of men clearly dominant in this case, too. Kinsey claims that in the countryside almost every other man has regular sexual contact with animals, in some areas even up to two-thirds. And the most frequent sexual partners are cows, a German study suggests.

One of these contemporary "*Kühgyer*" is the self-avowed sodomite Peter Stierli (in English—"little bull"). He used this very appropriate pseudonym in a featured debate in a Swiss news magazine a few years ago. Peter Stierli is probably what Hirschfeld would have referred to as a "distress zoophile": someone who has professional contact with animals and who "as soon as other opportunities for sexual relaxation . . . are lacking" seeks the closeness and affection of animals. Peter Stierli was introduced to sodomy in his youth while working as a farmhand. He was immediately "fascinated" without actively taking part in it. It was only when Stierli was eighteen and his girlfriend left him that he had his first sexual intercourse with a cow. "It was wonderful," he reports retrospectively, "I cycled home cheering."

Asked what makes cows so attractive to him, Stierli explains that on the one hand there's something very "warm, beautiful, and comfortable" about these animals; on the other hand they also have "attributes of an object" that you can use whenever the mood strikes. "That is . . . the natural order. Humans have always subjugated animals. It doesn't matter whether you milk or hump a cow." These statements coincide with Magnus Hirschfeld's assessment. According to the sexologist the cow is "an object for masturbation" for the zoophile. In the estimation of most zoophiles they rank no higher than the "artificial imitation of a woman in the shape of a blow-up rubber doll. "

Peter Stierli indulged his passion for cows for many years. But in January 1997 he was eventually caught red-handed by the police in a cowshed near Zurich and subsequently put on trial. He was, however, not sentenced for copulating with a cow. The Swiss district judge before whom Stierli appeared decided that Stierli had always treated the animals with great "gentleness." He agreed with the defense lawyer, who had explained that the accused had always spent several hours on foreplay with the cow. He argued that the sodomized animals had been treated better than many a human, which was why no animal abuse offense had been committed. The only offense for which Stierli was prosecuted was trespassing.

Although sexual intercourse with cows (as well as any other form of bestiality) is illegal in Canada, New Zealand, many U.S. states, and all Australian states and territories, it is not considered a crime in many European countries, as long as there's no evidence that the animal has been tortured. There, sexual contact with animals is limited only by the animal protection act and, in cases where the animal belongs to someone else, by laws pertaining to trespassing and property damage. This puts modern European jurisdiction in line with the opinion of honorary medical consultant Hirschfeld, who as early as 1930 argued conclusively and drily: "The animal protection act concerns only abuse cases, and intercourse cannot be labeled as such. The animal may even feel a pleasurable sensation. None of them has commented on it so far."

SINCE COWS cannot, as Hirschfeld remarked, express themselves, at least not in a way that humans understand, it is left to singers and poets to take up the subject of cattle love and shine light on it from the male and, more rarely, the female perspective. It's quite striking that the male desire for cows is often very thinly veiled. The old cowboy tune "I'm Bound to Follow the Longhorn Cows," for example, is about the longing of a poor American cowherd who longs to marry his great love or at least spend a few romantic hours with her. But his economic situation forces him to spend his life with a herd of cows and a bunch of other cowboys:

> One night way up in Kansas, I had a pleasant dream,
> I dreamed I'se back in Texas, boys, down by some
>     pleasant stream.
> My love was right beside me, boys, she'd come to go my
>     bail,
> But I woke up broken-hearted with a yearling by the tail.

This stanza clearly involves a dream, and since our subconscious is known to express itself in our dreams without inhibition, a brief interpretation based on depth psychology may be in order. First, however, we have to state one fact that is rather obvious but is normally omitted in the popular westerns that have shaped our image of the American cowboy. From the point of view of sexuality, the situation of a Swiss mountain farmer who stays up on the alp for the long summer months is not that different from that of a cowboy who spends all summer on the endless plains. They presumably both suffer from pent-up sexual urges and are left with what Hirschfeld calls "only three possibilities" to deal with them: homosexuality, zoophilia, or masturbation.

There's no obvious reason why the relative frequency of zoophilia should be lower on the Great Plains than in the place Alfred Kinsey collected his data. On the contrary—you could be tempted to think that it's higher in the solitude of nature than elsewhere, making the lonesome cowboy jump at the opportunity. It seems the cliché of the tough guy who loves his horse (only platonically, of course) and who will walk through fire (or ride through water, like Howard Hawks's hero Matt Garth in Red River) for the cows in his charge just doesn't match the image of a zoophile. We are simply unwilling to grant our lonesome western hero a sex life, least of all one that is way off the mainstream.

Even the first lines of "I'm Bound to Follow the Longhorn Cows" are subliminally marked by unfulfilled sexuality. The cowboy boasts he can catch a bolt of lightning with his lasso and "ride" on it. He reports to have difficulty calming down the cows at night. Every time he has got "them bedded down," a storm arises, and "fire plays on their horns." In this stanza, the thunderstorm finally discharges itself. The singer is too polite to express what exactly happens between the cowboy and the calf. But there's no doubt that in the heat of the night the cowboy has mistaken the young cow for his lover and has gotten close enough to grab her tail, if he hasn't fallen asleep with the cow in the first place. The fact that the cowboy's thoughts of his lover didn't make him reach for the teats of the calf but for the very body part that, apart from the horns maybe, most closely resembles a man's penis speaks volumes with respect to the above-mentioned possibilities of finding a solution to what Hirschfeld calls the "sexual needs of herdsmen." It logically follows that in the next and last stanza the cowboy gives short shrift to his lover's wish to get married and suggests she marry someone else. He wants to stay with his cows and the other cowboys until death do them part:

> My girl must cheer up courage and choose some other
> one,
> For I'm bound to follow the longhorn cows until my race
> is run.

The 1925 silent movie *Go West* by American comic actor Buster Keaton tells a very similar story. Keaton plays a lonesome cowboy with the telling name Friendless who makes the acquaintance of a cow named Brown Eyes who also lives on the margins of (cattle) society. He frees Brown Eyes, of a pebble that has become stuck in her hoof. In turn, she saves him from a wild bull shortly after. From that moment on, the two are inseparable. Keaton loans his blanket to the cow at night. When he is ordered to brand her, he doesn't have the heart to go through with the cruel procedure and instead uses milk foam and his razor to shave the farmer's sign into her hide.

Brown Eyes and Friendless in Buster Keaton's 1925 film *Go West*.

Only at the end of the movie do we realize what an extraordinary place the cow has come to take in Friendless's heart. Having saved the farmer from financial ruin, through luck rather than skill, Keaton is granted the classic wish that people with power and money tend to offer in exceptional cases: "My home and anything I have are yours for the asking." Friendless doesn't need to think very hard: "I want her," he says, pointing toward the farmer's pretty daughter with whom he has already been trying to flirt. The daughter looks coy and flattered, the farmer as if he might have to reconsider his overly generous offer. But then the lonesome cowboy's wish is explained. He didn't mean the daughter but the cow Brown Eyes, who (hidden from the spectator's and the farmer's view) was standing behind the farmer's daughter. The last shot is of Friendless and Brown Eyes, happily reunited on the backbench of a cabriolet chauffeured by the farmer, driving into the fade-out as if on their way to their honeymoon.

HERE AGAIN, the relationship of man and cow is only hinted at in a playfully flirtatious way. There are (as is typical for movies of that era) no actual sexual encounters. As the screenwriter, director, and leading actor, Buster Keaton remained within the limits of certain principles of the genre. He also worked against the backdrop of puritanical sexual ethics that were hostile toward the body and would hardly condone an explicit discussion of the topic. The Austrian poet Ernst Jandl had much more freedom and took many more liberties when he wrote the poem "pissing cow" sixty years later:

> cow piss in an elegant arc
> escaping the cow's body;
> the ordinary groom trembling, used to
> screwing mares; watching the pasture pageant
> of delicately splayed out cow tails that must not
> be splashed by urine, rips open
> his trouser zipper from which bulges his
> reproductive organ welded on by his grandchildren-crazy
> mother as a guarantee for a foal, a little calf to bring
> > home to her
> from a successful educational journey.

The protagonist of this poem is sent on a strange "educational journey." Traditionally the so-called Grand Tour that was so popular with rich and aristocratic Europeans of the eighteenth and nineteenth centuries didn't lead to the countryside but to the great cities of art, mostly in France and Italy. The journey was meant to put the finishing touches on the cultural education of young men. In many cases though, the journey provided them with an opportunity to gain non-committal erotic experience before getting married and settling down for good.

Because of his standing—he is a simple "groom"—the erotic experience of the young man Jandl describes has so far been restricted to mares. Now, however, at the sight of a cow baring her backside to pee, he is suddenly overcome by the overwhelming desire to put the finishing touches on his gentlemanly education and finally mate with a cow. The (genetically unattainable) goal of his endeavor: to bring home a grandchild for his mother, a bastard cattle, or "a little calf."

The use of lowercase spelling throughout the German text is typical of Jandl. The heavy-handed syntax, by contrast, is rather unusual for his work. The numerous awkward constructions and participles make it sound like a direct translation from Ancient Greek or Latin. The "pissing cow" is indeed a kind of transliteration, the radically changed reproduction of an ancient myth that is so provocative that Gustav Schwab decided it was best not to include it in his collection *The Most Beautiful Legends of Classic Antiquity*: the story of Pasiphae.

PASIPHAE WAS the daughter of the sun god Helios and the Oceanid Perse. She was married to King Minos of Crete. But her greatest passion—a punishment for her husband who forgot to sacrifice the animal to the sea god Poseidon—was an impressive white bull. "There roamed in majestic aloofness a white bull of unparalleled beauty. Between his horns there was a single black spot, and this merely emphasized the exquisite pallor of his coat," the Roman poet Ovid extols.

In order to seduce this divine creature and engage in sexual pleasure with him, Pasiphae needs some kind of prosthesis—not a "welded-on" organ of reproduction like the farmhand in Jandl's poem but a wooden dummy, an artificial cow body in which she can hide and be mounted by the bull. Pasiphae commissions the legendary inventor and sculptor Daedalus to construct the artificial cow. The German dramatist Botho Strauß recounts her pleading and longing in his mythological play *The Park*, in which the scene is shifted to a city park in Germany:

> I'm only a poor woman, who is in heat.
> I'm crying out—everything in me cried out—
> For this white beast.
> I'm tormenting myself over him, I'm all on fire.
> My genitals are as plump as a cow's
> My sleek rosy skin is all swollen with suspicious
> Looking bulges; sticky slime, not the discharge of a
>     woman; but rather of a cow!
> My breath tastes hot and fetid, like a cow's
> . . .
> Make the backside of a cow for me!
> I couldn't stand it if he didn't come to me.
> The way I'm made, so human and skinny, I'll never
> Excite him.
> . . .
> Daedalus, I feel so ashamed; why am I confined
> Inside this cramped female body?

Daedalus does as he is told and constructs a sort of Trojan cow from maple wood spanned by calf leather. According to Michael Brackmann, Daedalus can therefore claim to be "the inventor of the mating stall"—today, very similar contraptions are used in insemination stations to stimulate breeding bulls. Daedalus's deception works, and the bull is bewitched by the cow mock-up. Nine months later Pasiphae gives birth to a man-cow bastard, the Minotaur, for whom Daedalus will later build the famous labyrinth as a secure place of concealment. Ovid concludes that female passion knows no bounds and may occasionally even be perverse. But it will always find fulfillment, something that should suit men:

> These are a few examples of woman's uncontrollable passion. It is ten times fiercer than ours and full of madness. So be of good faith and you cannot fail. Not one in ten thousand will offer resistance.

We know now that it's genetically impossible for sexual intercourse between humans and cattle to result in composite creatures like the Minotaur. However, producing such hybrids in a laboratory has recently become quite possible. In the spring of 2008, British stem cell researchers at Newcastle University created the first human-cow hybrid embryos. Although they were destroyed after three days and five cell divisions, the indignant outcry that followed the publication of the experiments in the media was huge. The Scottish cardinal Keith O'Brien lamented the trials as a "monstrous attack on human rights" and referred to them as "experiments of Frankenstein proportions." And a fearful question in the tabloid *Bild* read: "Are scientists crafting a new Minotaur, the legendary composite creature of animal and human?"

It's interesting to see that, despite all scientific progress, the cultural unease toward the physical amalgamation of human and cattle is hardly less pronounced today than it was two thousand years ago. Even Lyle Armstrong, the scientist who was responsible for breeding the hybrid embryos, had to admit that his experiments might seem "a bit repulsive at first sight," adding, "but you have to understand that we use only very, very little information from the cow."

# THE EYE

NO OTHER body part of the cow is subject to as much derision and criticism as her eyes. The very sensory organ that in the Western world is perceived to be the mirror of a living being's soul or character is the one that most people nowadays view as ugly and dull in cows. You won't score by complimenting someone on his or her "cow eyes." But that wasn't always the case. And the change in perception of the cow's eye over the past millennia perhaps reflects our changing relationship with the cow.

IN CONTRAST to us, the ancient Greeks viewed being cow-eyed as an ideal of beauty. The great Hera, Zeus's wife and thus the highest goddess, was honored with the flattering nickname *Boopis*, "the cow-eyed one." Homer, for instance, repeatedly refers to Hera with that epithet. And that is how we encounter her in most antique sculptures: large and imposing, with wide-open, roundish eyes that overlook more or less graciously her husband's many sexual escapades. Hera herself was as loyal to her husband as a docile cow. She was considered the patroness of women and monogamous marriage. One of her most famous temples was located on the island of Euboea, where she was said to have married Zeus. The name of this island, too, is a reflection of the beauty of Hera's eyes: it means "good for cows."

The shift toward a more negative meaning of the epithet started in Roman times, with the letters of the sharp-tongued orator and politician Marcus Tullius Cicero. To his friend Atticus, Cicero repeatedly called a Roman woman named Clodia, the sister of his archenemy Publius Clodius Pulcher, *Boopis*, once even *Boopis nostra*, "our cow-eyed one." This may at first sound like unfettered praise of Clodia's beauty—the great Roman poet Catullus had, after all, written some of his most passionate poems for the lady. But maybe Cicero had something completely different in mind. According to Greek mythology, Hera (called Juno by the Romans) was actually not just Zeus's wife—she was also his sister. By comparing his political enemy's sister to Hera, Cicero probably meant to imply not only that she had two divinely beautiful cow eyes but also that she, like the cow-eyed goddess, had an incestuous relationship with her brother.

AS SOON as Early New High German had established itself as the standard language in the German-speaking world, the notion of beautiful cow eyes was a thing of the past. Numerous sayings from the Late Middle Ages proclaim that the eyes of cows and calves express stupidity and wretchedness, most noticeably when the animals face death. "His eyes are crossed like those of a slaughtered calf" was a common expletive in the sixteenth century. The Calvinist writer Johann Baptist

Fischart railed against a Catholic priest who had fallen to his knees: "Why does the parson suddenly look as pitiful and compassionate as a slaughtered calf?" The irritated look that cows put on when faced with changes in their familiar surroundings was also seen as the epitome of gawking and ignorant stupidity. "For we have eyes," the Reformist Martin Luther lectured, "like a cow looking at a new gate." This was echoed by his contemporary Jakob Böhme, who said that we humans look "at ourselves and at God's creation like a cow looks at a new barn door."

With the emergence of modern psychology in the nineteenth and early twentieth centuries, the cow's facial expression even became pathologized. The 1927 *Klinisches Wörterbuch* (Clinical dictionary) by Otto Dornblüth, a standard German reference book for medical terminology at the time, lists *boopis* or "cow eye" as a pathological condition. According to Dornblüth, the term refers to a symptom of hysteria that manifests itself in a "deliberately soulful" facial expression. Hysteria was a condition that was diagnosed almost exclusively in women. The term is derived from the Greek *hystera* or "womb." In the Middle Ages, it was assumed that the womb was a kind of animal, an itinerant organ, which in the absence of sexual intercourse went wandering around the woman's body, thereby triggering the symptoms in question. Although Sigmund Freud didn't believe in the idea of a wandering womb, he still assumed that hysteria could be cured "by marriage and normal sexual intercourse." Lack of sexual fulfillment, a problem that probably affected Hera, who was neglected by her husband, was now interpreted as the root cause of a mysterious affliction. A Greek goddess can hardly sink any lower.

Modern conventional medicine eventually degraded the cow eye to a profane object of study. Easy to come by (from slaughterhouses) and structurally more or less identical to the human visual organ, it's ideally suited for high school biology classes and for medical students who want to investigate the eye's anatomy up close and personal on the dissecting table. The surrealist filmmaker Luis Buñuel was one of the people who appreciated this similarity. His first movie, *An Andalusian Dog* (1929), starts with the vivisection of a wide-open eye that's being cut in half by the director with a freshly sharpened razor. The scene seems to suggest that it's the eye of a young woman. In reality it's the eye of a dead cow, which has been distorted by overexposure.

However, knowing this hardly reduces the almost palpable pain that the image can trigger in the viewer. Buñuel and his coauthor Salvador Dalí chose to attack the key organ of the cinema, the eye, of all things. Like the cow eye, the viewing habits of the movie goers were "dissected." Dalí later remarked, with a touch of his trademark vanity, that *An Andalusian Dog* had "ruined ten years of pseudo-intellectual postwar avant-gardism in a single evening." "That foul thing which is figuratively called abstract art fell at our feet, wounded to the death, never to rise again, after having seen a girl's eye cut with a razor-blade." The vivisection scene certainly put an end to an innocent, "cow-eyed" view of film as a medium.

ON THE whole, the appreciation of the cow eye appears to have been sinking continuously for over two thousand years. The ancient Romans, who started vilifying the cow eye, were also the first ones to engage in systematic cattle breeding. And it seems that the more cows are an integral part of systematic agricultural exploitation, the less inclined we are to consider them as more than hide, flesh, and bones, or, in other words, as beings with a soul—the window to which are, of course, the eyes. At the beginning of the nineteenth century, English essayist William Hazlitt noted that in the case of "animals that are made use of as food" we should "not leave the form standing to reproach us with our gluttony and cruelty."

When we look a cow in the eye, we take her seriously as a fellow creature, as a being that can reproach us or make us feel guilty. We may even discover the secret that is, according to philosopher Martin Buber, communicated through the eyes of animals alone: "Without needing cooperation of sounds or gestures, most forcibly when they rely wholly on their glance, the eyes express the mystery in its natural prison, the anxiety of becoming." If, however, we dismiss the look in a cow's eyes as dull and dumb, if we shrug off the look in the eyes of a slaughtered calf as pathetic, and consider an open, soulful look as pathological and calculating, then it's undoubtedly easier to look upon the cow as soulless meat stock whose only importance lies in providing us with food.

So once again it's left to the writers to remind us of the loveliness of cow eyes. After all, beauty is not only found in the eye of the cow but mostly in the eye of the beholder. In his *Tierskizzenbüchlein* (Little book of animal sketches), Hellmut von Cube, for example, glorifies the cow eye as the seat and epitome of the peaceable serenity that we so admire in cows:

> The tranquility of cows, however, . . . is concentrated
> in the look of their round, dark eyes. The gentleness,
> patience, and wonder in them are just exterior signs
> and proclamations. Like the dark, meandering paths

leading into a huge, unknown grotto, they reveal the deep, unspeakable peace inside the earth, the way that a few words can often reveal a human being . . . Those to whom these eyes have revealed themselves begin to understand the look of flowers, a look that expresses the same thing, only more subtle and quiet and remote and without the sadness inherent in all conscious creatures.

In his 1983 novel *The Cow*, Beat Sterchi demonstrates that there are ways of interpreting the look of a slaughtered calf empathically as an expression of great worldly wisdom and resignation. Having been humiliated by the management again and again, the workers of the slaughterhouse where most of the novel is set remember the strengthening and community-building power of cattle blood. They decide to conduct a libation ritual, a kind of archaic communion. They lead a cow—not a modern meat breed but an Eringer, a traditional Swiss fighting cow—into the slaughterhouse and decorate her with flowers. Then they kill the animal using a technique reminiscent of the Jewish slaughtering method of shechita or its Islamic counterpart dhabiha—by stabbing it in the carotid artery without first stunning it:

> The little Eringer . . . mooed feebly, and her eyes lightened as they looked at the men standing in front of her. The cow stood and bled, and it was as though she knew the long history of her kind . . . It was as though this little cow understood the scorn and contempt that had been leveled at her subjugated species since that time, but as though she could still hear, from the back of her skull . . . the echo of her ancestors' hoofbeats as they thundered over the

steppes, like storm clouds, in their great herds, and it was as though this rushing and roaring showed itself unmistakably in the humility in the eyes of the little cow.

Finally, at the center of Martin Mosebach's 2005 novel *Das Beben* (The tremor) is a detailed analysis of the holy cows of India. The novel's protagonist has fled from his unfaithful lover and gone to India. He steps off the plane at Udairpur airport and walks into the terminal building, where he promptly encounters a zebu, the Indian version of the domestic cow. He is immediately taken by the cow but mostly captivated by her look:

> There was something childlike in her gentle eyes. They were more closely set together than in European cows. Her head was small and slender and her eyes slightly slanted. The cow didn't gawk. I do like the protruding European cow eye, too—that meaningful Juno look; but here I saw, possibly heightened by the noble, light-gray color, something of the piety and patience of a donkey.

As if he had read Martin Buber's analysis of the look of animals that can speak volumes, the narrator soon comes to the conclusion that the pure, disinterested look of the cow is the expression of a secret—that with their eyes, cows can enable humans to share in a transcendent sphere that can't be articulated. He lets us know that he has "through the figure of the holy cow experienced as much holiness as we can possibly experience on earth. Nothing abstract, but a big, living animal—larger than humans and impervious to their calculating and analytic way of thinking—that speaks to them through its eyes alone." The more the narrator thinks about holy cows, the more he understands that all the lyrical things he has said about the cow and her eyes actually also apply to the lover he left behind in Germany. At the same time, he also realizes that the Western world in general and his lover in particular are simply no longer prepared to accept cow-eyed compliments: "No pointer to Homer or Hera the *boopis*," he writes, "would be an excuse if she suddenly realized that I had thought of her in connection with a cow."

SO WHY does the narrator in Mosebach's novel find it so difficult to communicate the beauty of the cow-eye look to his lover? Or, to put it the other way around, why do so many people so easily dismiss the cow's eye as ugly?

For one thing, there is the actual eyeball. Cows normally have dark irises (and not, for instance, bright blue or green eyes), and so their pupils are much harder to discern than human pupils. The white sclera surrounding the pupil is often altogether invisible; only occasionally, when cows try to look at something outside their field of vision, when they are frightened or nervous, or when they try to break away, will they roll their eyeballs in their sockets, briefly revealing the whites. With a bit of goodwill and keen poetic perception, such large dark eyes lend themselves to an interpretation as "caves" that lead deep into earth's interior or to the very bottom of one of the world's great secrets. And yet, in a society that predominately appreciates a bold, penetrating, analytical look, it can just as easily be interpreted as naive, hopelessly romantic, or simply stupid. Adding to that is the fact that the cow eye protrudes slightly from its socket, giving the cow a googly-eyed look. When seen in humans, the phenomenon is often interpreted as a symptom for an ophthalmic, mental, or thyroid disease.

Apart from that, where the eyes are located on a cow's head might also contribute to our perception of the cow's look as inferior. Martin Mosebach has pointed out that the eyes of the Indian zebu are set closer together than those of domestic European cattle. Anyone trying to meet the eyes of our indigenous cow in the same way as we do with other humans—that is, from the front—will almost invariably be disappointed. When looking at cows from the front, the viewer is presented primarily with a wide, horned forehead and a wet nose, with which the cow will probably nuzzle the viewer's face. Our urge to meet the steady stare of a pair of eyes that are parallel and dominate the front of the face goes unfulfilled.

So when we see the cow's eye as ugly, we presumably apply inappropriate—that is, human—standards. And yet, there are good, even vital reasons for the design and position of the cow's eyes. As cows are animals that run and flee, they have to be able to react to the tiniest changes in their environment, even those that take place behind them. The position of their eyes gives them about a 270-degree view; in order to get a 360-degree view of their surroundings and to scan them for suspicious changes, they have to move their head only a little bit.

However, the fact that the fields of vision of their eyes overlap makes it extremely hard for cows to estimate distances. Their retinas also lack the macula, or "yellow spot" that's responsible for focusing within a given field of view. Cows see the world relatively blurred. The metal cattle guards often installed on mountain roads seem like insurmountable abysses to them. At times, glaring white lines on the road are enough to give them the illusion of spatial depth. Their color perception is also limited. Cows see mostly colors in the yellow-green spectrum, which is why they show a great deal of curiosity or aggression when faced with unsuspecting hikers wearing bright yellow raincoats or lime-green T-shirts.

On the other hand, cows have much better night vision than humans and sensory faculties that are superior to ours in some respects. They have excellent hearing, and their sense of smell is approximately fifteen times as acute as ours. Their sense of taste, too, is very pronounced, which is why cows sometimes refuse fodder or water for reasons that we don't understand. So their sensory perception isn't more limited or duller than ours. As the environmental philosopher Jakob von Uexküll would put it, cows simply live in a cognitive "bubble" different from ours.

Very few people are privileged to dip into the bubble of cows. Animal psychologist Temple Grandin claims to be one of them. In her book *Animals in Translation*, she argues that cows perceive the world "like autistic savants." People with this condition (Grandin is among them) have one or more areas of outstanding expertise, ability, or brilliance but often experience considerable difficulties in mastering everyday situations. They are extremely detail oriented and notice even the smallest changes that would pass most people by. Presumably it's the inability to prioritize the flood of perceptions and to ignore certain types of information that makes dealing with daily life so difficult for autistic people.

According to Temple Grandin, cows are in a similar situation. They too constantly perceive the world in all its overwhelming richness of detail. If they encounter something they're unfamiliar with, they'll consider it, for the time being, a potential danger. That's why they will be afraid of a raincoat accidentally left on a fence and refuse to walk past it. Or they will, as in Martin Luther's and Jakob Böhme's descriptions, stand in front of a new gate with eyes wide with astonishment.

THE 1981 oil painting *The Innocent Eye Test* by American painter Mark Tansey illustrates the great importance we humans attach to the look of the cow's eye, the differences between human and animal sensory perceptions notwithstanding. As is typical of Tansey's work, the painting is almost photorealistic. At the same time, the dominance of monochrome gray tones gives the picture the sepia appearance of an old photograph and seems to move the represented scene away from the present. However, the conventional suits that the people in the picture are wearing could well be modern-day ones.

A cow is depicted at the center of the painting. The setting appears to be a museum, where a group of bespectacled researchers are trying to decipher the secret of the cow-eye look, testing its "innocence." Three of the gentlemen are to the left of the cow, three to the right. One of them is holding a notebook and a pen to document her behavior; another one has a wet mop at the ready to clean away any possible mess the cow might make. The two researchers closest to the cow hold a large cloth to unveil another painting—a picture within the picture. That painting is one of the most famous depictions of cattle in the history of occidental art: *The Bull* by the Dutch Baroque painter Paulus Potter. In the background is another picture that could be of interest to cows, a haystack by Impressionist Claude Monet. Whoever curated the depicted exhibition certainly had a soft spot for cattle.

Mark Tansey's *The Innocent Eye Test* (1981).

However, the scientists are oblivious to the masterpieces around them. They eagerly look at the cow. Her ears are pricked up, and she is attentively looking at the canvas. The young bull in the canvas seems to be looking at the cow in front of him. Tansey obviously captured the moment just after the Paulus Potter painting has been revealed, so we don't get to know how the cow will react. Will she take an interest in the young bull, because she mistakes his picture for the real thing? Or does she have an innocent eye and, like a young child, can see only two-dimensional colored areas on the canvas but not the three-dimensional world that these areas represent?

The term "innocent eye" in the painting's title goes back to the English painter and art theorist John Ruskin. In the mid-nineteenth century, he had called on his colleagues to regain "the innocence of the eye; that is to say, a sort of childish perception of these flat stains of color, merely as such, without consciousness of what they signify, as a blind man would see them if suddenly gifted with sight."

At the same time, the scene is reminiscent of an art story from ancient Greece, of the most famous work of the sculptor Myron. He is said to have created not only a discus thrower, a pentathlete, a dog, an ant, and a cricket, as well as many other works, but also an artificial cow. The cow sculpture was allegedly so realistic that all other beings thought it was alive. A lion allegedly tried to tear the cow to pieces. A bull tried to mount her. A calf came to drink from her udder, while a herd of cows passing by was happy to include her in their midst. A farmer wanted to yoke her to a plow, and a thief tried to steal her. A horsefly sat down on her back and tried to bite the stone, and poor cow-eyed Hera became jealous, because she mistook the cow for one of her husband's lovers. Even Myron himself is said to have mistaken her for one of his herd. Paulus Potter, the creator of *The Bull*, was of course at a disadvantage compared with the sculptor, as he was restricted to two dimensions. Nevertheless, Potter's contemporaries are said to have found the cow paintings so realistic that they felt they could actually smell the cows. If the Dutch master's work was indeed as mimetic as that of old Myron, the cow in Tansey's painting should react as enthusiastically to the sight of the young bull as the animals, humans, and ancient gods did to *bucula Myronis*.

At the end of the day, the cloven-hoofed protagonists in Tansey's picture are just a piece of art, animals on a canvas. And that's what makes *The Innocent Eye Test* so complex. Why would Tansey's deceptively realistic-looking cow see more than the deceptively realistic-looking bull in Paulus Potter's painting? And what do we see when we look at the picture? Do we see a cow looking at a bull that's looking at a cow looking at a bull? Maybe the bull can see us too. Do we even see a bull or a cow or a group of scientists? Or is all we see, after looking at it long enough, just a cluster of flat splashes of color? Are we possibly the actual objects of study in this strange examination of the "innocent eye"? We stand in front of the painting, puzzled, ruminating about these questions with big, round, astonished eyes.

# HAPPINESS THROUGH
# RUMINATION

A LOW SKY over the grayish-green hills, heavy with rain. A small pond, lush meadows. In the foreground four cows are trotting along a country road; a fifth one is grazing a ways off. A man with a stick and a bicycle follows behind. "Rush Hour—Ireland," reads the caption on this picture postcard, implying that that's how tranquil Irish country roads look at the beginning of rush hour. And that's what it's like when cows are in a rush: very, very slow. "It had felt blasphemous, when someone once said to me in Germany, 'The roads belong to the automobile,'" Heinrich Böll notes with horror in his *Irish Journal*. "In Ireland I was often tempted to say, 'the roads belong to the cow . . .'" It's a happy country with happy cows.

Like almost no other domestic animal, the cow symbolizes peace and tranquility. Goats are considered uptight. Pigs grunt and wallow in mud. The bleating of sheep gets on our nerves. Mares are vicious, especially toward other mares. Cats are moody, dogs aggressive. And chickens are notoriously

# RUSH HOUR-IRELAND

Cows line up during rush hour in Ireland, according to this postcard.

nervous and flighty. Cows, by contrast, just stand stoically in the meadows and seem unaffected by inclement weather conditions and life's adversities. No wonder humans keep casting jealous glances across the fence and project their longing for a relaxed lifestyle onto the animals on the other side. "In no animal is there to be met with . . . a more humble and pliant disposition," the English wood engraver Thomas Bewick wrote in his *General History of Quadrupeds* as early as 1790. Some 130 years later, the English poet and novelist D.H. Lawrence commented favorably on the "cowy oblivion," the "cowy passivity," the "cowy silence," and the "cowy peace" of a black cow named Susan, which he kept on his ranch near Taos, New Mexico, and took particular pleasure in milking early every morning: "How can I equilibrate myself with my black cow Susan?" he repeatedly wondered. "Or even, if you prefer the word, to get in harmony with her?"

At about the same time, the German poet Joachim Ringelnatz praised the calm with which cows drop dung in the
morning and munch while doing nothing more than chase
away a fly with a twitch of their tail, calling it the epitome of
heaven on earth.

How paradisiac this is!
Warm fattening bellies steaming,
Wiggling mouths, with snot a-gleaming,
the meadow's champagne bubbles kiss.

They promenade with bovine grandeur,
A fence their liberty curtails.
A touch of nerves, mixed with the splendor,
tucked in the tassels of their tails.

In the eyes of German nature writer Hellmut von Cube, this
majestic tranquility is the very essence of domesticated cattle:

As birds are made of movement, cows are made of calmness. Everything about them is calm: the large, economic
lines, the stolid surfaces and bulges, their step-by-step
grazing, their heads with which they look backwards in
wonder, even the twitch of their tails with which they
chase away horseflies. Whereas calmness is a temporary state for a lurking cat, for an ibex who sits looking
intently and immobile for hours, or for a frog resting
on a sunny water lily leaf, for cows it is their very nature.
That's why they are more soothing than any other animal,
why watching them graze is a balsamic blessing.

According to von Cube it's not simply that cows are calm in themselves—their calmness also transfers to the observer. Merely seeing the grazing animals has the effect of a healing balm, a "balsamic blessing" for the retina and nervous soul of civilization-stricken humans, letting them take part in the animals' enviable contentment.

This positive attitude toward the calming effect of cows has carried over into our modern consumer society. The ads of the Swiss Milk Producers' Association, for instance, have for several years now featured the association's mascot, the cow Lovely. She shows Swiss milk drinkers various yoga positions, which are meant to transfer the calmness of the four-legged bovine to its two-legged emulators. Nowadays there are several humorous German books with titles like *Yoga for Cows* or *Picking Clover*, in which cartoon cows demonstrate yoga positions called "opening the gate," "greeting the farmer," or "holding the milk bucket." For a while, stressed office workers could relax by downloading the sound of a cow herd from the homepage of the British Organic Milk Suppliers Cooperative. The site prompted them to do some meditative mooing with the cows: "Sing or say the word 'moo.' Take your time and let the word linger for an entire exhalation . . . If you are in an open-space office, it is OK to just moo internally." The cow, it seems, is not only the epitome of calmness but also the ideal symbol of the postmodern wellness society.

That cows are normally so exceptionally calm is first and foremost a biological necessity. Cattle are, after all, originally prey—and for animals who play the role of the hunted rather than the hunter, it's important not to show any signs of panic, pain, or weakness that would attract a predator's attention. The cat that Hellmut von Cube observed is a predator by nature. It sits still only to convert its rest energy into speed and to seize its unwary victim quick as lightning. The ibex, staring quietly, can in a pinch flee from its enemies into the most remote mountain regions. The frog jumps and disappears under the water's surface when it sees a bird of prey approaching. Cows, by contrast, usually move around in a terrain in which they can make headway no faster than their pursuers. However restless they might feel inside, they can't show it to the world. That's why, as von Cube puts it, calmness is their "very nature." Composure is their survival strategy.

Apart from that, a cow's daily grind consists mostly of what seems to be an extremely relaxing, almost hypnotically soothing activity: rumination. This special technique of food processing allows cows to use the cellulose contained in the grass fiber—something mammals with only one stomach can't digest—as a nutrient. On the one hand, cows can do this "work" (unlike grazing) easily while lying down comfortably, which is why when ruminating they sometimes radiate the epicurean contentment of ancient Romans during a feast. On the other hand, they take an enchanting amount of time to chew the cud. Cows spend up to nine hours a day regurgitating food that has been stored in the rumen, mincing these morsels with forty to sixty chewing movements and swallowing them again. They make up to thirty thousand chewing movements a day, so the likelihood that a cow you see in a meadow is busy ruminating is pretty high.

A pasture thick with grass and flowers, lush and bright,
Dotted with horned heads hove into sight,
Divinely beautiful, a world of peace and calm.

I watched the gentle rumination,
Its graceful sound was my soul's balm
And filled my heart with joy and great elation.
So lovely to behold
How they, with eyes half-closed or shut quite tight,
Do savour the green juice with sensuous delight.

These are the first lines of Barthold Heinrich Brockes's poem "Die Heerde Kühe" (The herd of cows). There are obviously several things about rumination that make the poet rejoice. For one thing, all cows in the herd are doing the same thing more or less in synchronicity. At the same time, each of them is totally focused on itself—that is, busily ruminating the contents of her stomach. It's hard to imagine a more harmonious relationship between individual and society. Secondly, the uniform, almost mantra-like sound of the cows' chomping jaws is a delight for the poet's ear; so the soothing sight of the cows is augmented by a hypnotic rhythm. Last but not least, there is, as the poet notes, a sensuous quality to this rhythmic sucking of the chewed-up roughage. To be lying in a meadow with your girlfriends, to nibble with relish the food that, as though you were still in the Garden of Eden, has wandered into your mouth "all by itself," the way Brockes describes rumination is indeed the epitome of earthly pleasures.

ALTHOUGH BROCKES caught a glimpse of the divine in all natural phenomena, let alone cows, the deeply religious aspect of rumination seems to have escaped him. Two hundred years later, the writer Robert Musil emphasized that respect: "When one passed the grazing-land high up on the mountain," he writes in his short story "Grigia," the cattle were still half asleep. In big, dim, white stony shapes they lay with their legs drawn in under them, their hindquarters drooping a little to one side. They did not look at the passers-by, nor after him, but imperturbably kept their faces turned toward the expected light, and their monotonously, slowly moving jaws seemed to be praying. Walking through the circle of them was like traversing some twilit, lofty sphere of existence, and when one looked back at them from above, the line formed by the spine, the hind legs and curving tail made them seem like a scattering of treble-signs.

Musil describes otherworldly, ancient creatures here. Like the huge rocks of a stone-age cult they lie in a circle, forming a sort of cow-body Stonehenge that seems both animated by an unnamed "lofty sphere of existence" and merged with the surrounding landscape. The cows, meanwhile, are "still half asleep." They are in an intermediate state, a kind of trance, similar to the animals that Brockes described. It is the otherworldly, semiconscious attitude taken by priestesses, oracles, and diviners when they want to communicate with superior powers. And indeed, the cows leisurely move their jaws as if in prayer.

Just to whom the cows pay homage remains unclear. Perhaps they pray to a holy cow. What's important is that the leisurely jaw movements that cows make with their mouths, at times half open, at times closed, are in a way reminiscent of the act of speaking. Not so much a loud, vocal utterance that carries far but more the kind of quiet inner dialogue that one tends to hold with oneself, or one's god, for that matter.

On the one hand, the verb *ruminate* means "to chew one's

cud"; on the other hand, it can also mean "to think about something profoundly." In Martin Luther's Latin writings, the word *ruminare* is often equivalent to "ponder in one's heart" or "meditate"—in other words, it denotes activities that, like modern-day yoga, are supposed to lead to harmony with God and the world, and thus to inner peace.

THE IDEA of equating rumination with inner, spiritual processes goes back to St. Augustine of Hippo. In his auto-biographic *Confessions* the early medieval church father interpreted the rumen as a symbol for memory and the unchewed, half-digested food stored within it as the good and bad memories that we can keep bringing up, as cows do with food, in our minds.

> We might say that the memory is a sort of stomach for the mind and that joy or sadness are like bitter or sweet food. When this food is committed to the memory, it is as though it had passed into the stomach where it can remain but also loses its taste. Of course it is absurd to suppose that the memory is like the stomach, but there is some similarity nonetheless . . . Perhaps these emotions are brought forward from the memory by the act of remembering in the same way as cattle bring up food from the stomach when they chew the cud.

According to Augustine, a memory of a past experience resembles predigested food in a cow's mouth: in principle it's still the same sad or happy event, the same grass. But when the experience or food is regurgitated from memory or the stomach, respectively, it suddenly all tastes different. Sorrows remembered are not quite as bitter, joys remembered not quite as sweet. And the grass too is not as fresh as it was a few hours ago when it was first eaten.

However, cows and humans are different in a fundamental way: humans crave diversity, both in their food and in their lives. Cows are, at least when we judge them by their unflappable composure, content with the eternal sameness of things. Humans long to have new experiences and to incorporate them into their memories. Cows can happily eat and ruminate grass all their lives. A person who spends nine hours a day contemplating and constantly rehashing the same issue probably suffers from obsessive-compulsive disorder. Cows, by contrast, can "remember" the same thing over and over without coming to any harm. If they had a craving for change, they would perhaps act like the cartoon cow in The Far Side that Gary Larson endowed with a human conscience (and the faculty of speech). The cow and her two companions are standing in a lush meadow. Unlike her fellow cows, who are happily dipping their mouths into "the meadow's champagne bubbles," she stands there stiff as a poker with her head raised, looking around with large, incredulous eyes, as if she has just awoken from years of sleep, and cries, "Hey, wait a minute! This is grass! We've been eating grass!"

The fact that cows don't seem to be aware of the monotony of their existence has led many thinkers to conclude that cows lack the faculty of memory altogether. The philosopher Friedrich Nietzsche interpreted this as the very secret of happiness in animals in general and cows in particular: they, unlike humans, don't constantly seek new experiences that they then have to digest intellectually but are happy to content themselves with the eternal recurrence of the same. In his Untimely

*Meditations* he allegorizes the advantages of a life perpetually lived in the moment:

> A human being may well ask an animal: "Why do you not speak to me of your happiness but only stand and gaze at me?" The animal would like to answer and say: "The reason is I always forget what I was going to say"—but then it forgot the answer too and stayed silent: so that the human being was left wondering.

The happiness of cows, Nietzsche suggests, can tragically not be conveyed to humans, because it consists precisely of the impossibility to put things into words: the thoughts escape before being voiced.

That's perhaps the Nietzsche quote that Belgian film director Agnès Varda had in mind, when in her film *A Hundred and One Nights* she has a cow explain the advantages of a poor memory to the elderly Michel Piccoli. Resting on a four-poster bed, the Black-and-White informs the old "Monsieur Cinema" that memories are dangerous. The only chance for our imagination lies in oblivion, because it allows us to cast off the shackles of traditional conventions. *Vive l'oubli!* she shouts: "Long live oblivion!" The contradiction that Nietzsche demonstrated to comic effect by having his happy animal remain silent has been miraculously resolved here. The cow is able to forget but at the same time is able to remember what she was going to say. Interestingly this scene alludes to another important cow sequence in film history. The name of the cow in *A Hundred and One Nights* is that of a film director, Luis Buñuel. In his 1930 masterpiece *The Golden Age*, another cow, quite calm and oblivious to the world around her, also makes herself comfortable on a bed. Her owner, in the meantime, clearly much less happy and less calm than the cow, reminisces about her far-away lover.

In his book *Thus Spoke Zarathustra*, Nietzsche became even more outspoken about the relationship between rumination, oblivion, and happiness. In the fourth section, he describes how the book's prophet and protagonist, who has turned away from humankind, finds refuge in the solitude of the mountains. Zarathustra is cold; he feels lonely. But all of a sudden, he is imbued with something warm and animate: "Already I am less alone," he thinks. "Unconscious companions and brethren rove around me; their warm breath toucheth my soul." It is, however, not "companions and brethren" who rove around him but female companions and sisters.

> When, however, he spied about and sought for the comforters of his loneliness, behold, it were kine there standing together on an eminence, whose proximity and smell warmed his heart. The kine, however, seemed to listen eagerly to a speaker, and took no heed of him who approached. When, however, Zarathustra was quite nigh unto them, then did he hear plainly a human voice spake in the midst of the kine, and apparently all of them had turned their heads toward the speaker.

It's the "voluntary beggar" to whom the cows are listening so attentively: a hermit who left behind first his possessions and then human society and is now trying to find salvation among cows. Like the person in *Untimely Meditations*, he has not yet given up hope that the cows might, against all odds, remember what they wanted to tell him. He even believes that he is just about to get an answer from them:

"What do I here seek?" answered he: "the same that thou seekest, thou mischief-maker; that is to say, happiness on earth. To that end, however, I would fain learn of these kine. For I tell thee that I have already talked half a morning unto them, and just now were they about to give me their answer. Why dost thou disturb them? Except we be converted and become as kine, we shall in no wise enter into the kingdom of heaven. For we ought to learn from them one thing: ruminating. And verily, although a man should gain the whole world, and yet not learn one thing, rumination, what would it profit him! He would not be rid of his affliction.

The voluntary beggar isn't just preoccupied with an ordinary affliction but with a "great affliction; that, however, at present is called *disgust*." The hermit is so disgusted with human society that he can only bear to be with cows. The only things that distinguish humankind are "avidity, bilious envy, careworn revenge," and "populace-pride." Tellingly, all of these characteristics could not exist without memory. Only those who constantly think about their neighbors' property can be consumed with greed and envy. Only those who constantly remember past injustices are obsessed with revenge. Only those who dwell upon deeds accomplished a long time ago show excessive pride.

They chew with leisure; they slouch around in the sun and brood about neither the past nor the future: cows live in the nirvana of the absolute present. They have obviously reached the blissful state that otherwise only Zarathustra, the "victor of all great disgust" has attained. He has managed to accept the perpetual recurrence of eternal sameness as a basic condition of life. That's why the voluntary beggar attempts to approximate the cows' nature as closely as possible by idling and persistently crunching grains. That's why he views the cows as his dearest female friends and teachers, "one excepted whom I hold still dearer" as he clarifies in conclusion. "Thou thyself are good, O Zarathustra, and better even than a cow!" All those who never meet Zarathustra can at least find consolation in the fact that his representatives roam the earth in the billions. As the voluntary beggar puts it, "It is no longer true that the poor are blessed. The kingdom of heaven, however, is where the kine are."

# HERDING COWS

CONSIDERING THE heavenly happiness that ruminating cows exude, it's hardly surprising that humans have always sought out the presence of cows or envied those whose livelihood allows them to spend much of their time in the company of cattle. Not unlike stressed city dwellers today, the ancient Greeks projected their ideas about simplicity and carefree living onto the rural population. The verses with which they captured their longing soon grew so much in number that they made up a genre of their own—one that it made sense to name after those who looked after cows. And thus, *bucolic poetry*—poetry about the lives of cowherds— was born.

As the ancient Greeks knew only too well, people in the country have to deal with the same problems as those in cities—a fact that becomes obvious to city dwellers when they visit the countryside and are confronted with the harsh realities of the herders lives. Theocritus, the most important Greek pastoral poet, summed up this insight as early as the third century BCE in his poem "The Young Cowherd":

Shepherds, tell me the truth, "am I not beautiful?" Has
one of the gods, I wonder, made me on a sudden another
mortal? . . . And all the women along the mountain say
that I am handsome, and all of them love me; but the city
miss has not kissed me, but has run past me, because I
am a rustic; and she is not yet aware that beauteous Bac-
chus used to drive the calf in the valleys. Neither did she
know that Venus maddened after a herdsman, and tended
flock with him on the Phrygian mountains. And who was
Endymion? Was he not a herdsman? Yes, and him Selene
kissed as he fed his herds.

In short, bucolic poetry is not so much about the herdsmen's
work but mostly about their leisure. And according to Theocritus or later poets who sang the praise of herdsmen, such
as the Roman poet Virgil, the Renaissance poet Petrarch, or
the English court poet Sir Philip Sidney, that leisure consists
mainly of courtship. The cows (or goats or sheep) that are
herded are more like extras in the scene. On the one hand,
they are a welcome excuse to retire to the solitude of nature;
on the other hand, they make for an idyllic, steadily chewing,
and impassive-looking backdrop to the human hustle and
bustle. And if the herdsman's heart is full of sorrow, the cows
keep conveniently quiet to let him sing his song—or so English poet Alexander Pope suggests:

In the warm folds the tender flocks remain,
The cattle slumber on the silent plain,
While silent birds neglect their tuneful lays,
Let us, dear Thyrsis, sing of Daphne's praise.

The idea of country life as communicated in works like Theocritus's "Cowherd" or this eighteenth-century "Pastoral" is of course mainly a projection of metropolitan desires and longing. In the agricultural sector, keeping cows is considered a labor-intensive livelihood. There's a good reason for the old German folk saying, "One cow makes moo; many cows make ado" (*Eine Kuh macht Muh. Viele Kühe machen Mühe*). As Theocritus suggests, those who herd cows, who milk and feed them, hardly have time to canoodle with the womenfolk in the mountains, let alone compose poems in hexameter verse afterwards. This discrepancy might explain why from the seventeenth century onward the term *bucolic* was replaced by *pastoral* to refer to the poetry of shepherds rather than that of cowherds.

But even poems about herding cows have taken this contradiction into account. A recurring theme in bucolic poetry is precisely that constant conflict between desire and duty, between leisure and work, between pleasure and reality—in short, between the lover and the cow that must be herded. In his aubade "Das Kchühorn," the Monk of Salzburg, probably the most important love poet of the late Middle Ages, tells the story of a young couple who treat themselves to an extended nap "in the hay." Suddenly the sound of the cow horn unceremoniously catapults the maid out of the farmhand's arms and back into reality; this is a hallmark of the medieval aubade, which always recounts the rude awakening after coitus and the abrupt end of a rendezvous.

Spring's about
And the herdsmen strum:
Ho! Come out,

the time has come.
She wakes, night's end
is nigh, she wipes her brow,
goes to attend
the precious cow.

Of course the farmhand doesn't want to let his lover leave so soon. He's afraid that the cows might actually be male, human competitors who want the same kind of affection she has just given him. But the maid won't be sidetracked. The cows haven't been milked yet, she tells him, and if she were to arrive last, the other maids would tease her.

With udders full there stand the cows,
that's why I don't feel great.
Much mockery will I arouse,
if I again am late.

As is usual for bucolic poetry, the two lovers are members of the Third Estate—people of the lowest social stratum. We can assume that the milkmaid and the farmhand acted out the bucolic and erotic fantasies of the members of the Court of Salzburg, which is where the Monk of Salzburg lived and worked. "Das Kchühorn" sings of so-called lower love, which unlike courtly love involves "mere mortals" rather than a knight and a noblewoman. In contrast to courtly love it can also involve sexual fulfillment. Alas, there is not much time for that: the cows are waiting.

THE TWO lovers in the traditional Swiss folk song "Emmenthaler Kühreihen" (Emmenthal cow-calling song) face very similar problems. *She* spends the whole week with the cows up on the alpine pasture. *He* doesn't have time to visit her up there, and if he does get to see his darling once in a while, she has to milk the cows. But the girl knows only too well what to do in such cases:

> When I am supposed to be milking
> The cow won't stand still in her place.
> So I put my pail just beside me
> And entice the young farmhand with grace.

This is obviously no permanent solution. Successful gallivanting, just like profitable milking, needs time. The song ends with the logical conclusion that they should sell the cow and just keep the calf in order to finally have more time for each other:

> So we're selling the cow for a profit,
> But the calf we will keep with us here;
> Then others can milk every morning,
> And we can canoodle, my dear.

Like most antique cowherd poetry, like "Das Kchühorn" of the Monk of Salzburg, this text is written in dialogue form, a light-hearted exchange between a maid and a farmhand. However, as the title implies, this is a specific Swiss form of bucolic poetry, a cow-calling song.

Originally these *Kühreihen* probably developed from sounds with which the cowherds on the Alpine pastures called their animals to come for milking or to the trough. "When the cows follow the song of the herdsman and come running from all sides," writes Johann Gottfried Ebel in his *Schilderung der Gebirgsvölker der Schweitz* (Portrait of the mountain peoples of Switzerland),

> All those who have been grazing together or met one another on the way walk one behind the other in a *Reihe* or line. I suspect that that was the reason cow-calling songs that make them walk in a line were called *Kühereihen* or *Kuhreihen*.

The earliest-surviving version of a *Kühreihen* originates in the Appenzell region and was recorded in the sixteenth century. But a few decades later, cowherd songs had fallen into disrepute. The Basel doctor Theodor Zwinger reported in 1710 that these calls might not just affect cows but also human beings. The *Kühreihen* supposedly caused the many Swiss mercenary soldiers stationed abroad to suffer from acute homesickness, a phenomenon that was considered typically Swiss and therefore was also referred to as the Swiss disease or *mal de Suisse*.

"When *Kuhreihen* were played in Swiss regiments in France," writes Johann Gottfried Ebel, "the Alpine sons would burst into a flood of tears, and droves of them would be beset by such horrible homesickness, like an epidemic, that they deserted, or died, if they could not return to their fatherland." The "extraordinary effect of this Alpine music" was supposedly why the whistling or singing of *Kühreihen* by Swiss mercenary soldiers was forbidden "under pain of death." And that was not all—Ebel also reported that even Swiss cows got sick with *mal de Suisse* when someone sang a *Kühreihen* to them:

> When cows of Alpine breeding that have been removed from their country of birth hear this kind of song, images

of their former state seem to suddenly take shape in their brains too, triggering a kind of homesickness; they immediately throw their bent tail up in the air, start running, break down all fences and gates and are wild and frantic. This is why in the "St. Gallen" area, where cows bought in the "Appenzell" region often graze, it is forbidden to sing *Kuhreihen*.

No wonder Romantic artists, who had a weakness for the irrational, for all things magical and mysterious, were fascinated by the natural, almost bestial longing that the *Kühreihen* could supposedly trigger in humans and animals. What they saw

Thomas Gainsborough's *Landscape with a Woodcutter and Milkmaid* (1755, oil on canvas, private collection) shows how the bucolic ideal permeated visual art.

here were works of art that had an inexplicable and irresistible effect on the soul and made soldiers and cows throw off the shackles of civilization and breeding.

Like the legendary song of the Sirens, *Kühreihen* brought death to those who heard them. Philosopher Jean-Jacques Rousseau commented on the magic powers of these folk songs in his *Dictionary of Music*. Romantic composers like Robert Schumann, Felix Mendelssohn, and Richard Wagner paid homage to them in their musical works. And the poets Achim von Arnim and Clemens Brentano included a song about a soldier who follows the lure of the alpenhorn but is then court-martialed and shot, in their collection *Des Knaben Wunderhorn* (The youth's magical horn). It spread the myth of the fatal powers of *Kühreihen* and made them popular beyond Swiss borders: "Do not spare my young life / Shoot me so the blood splashes out / This I beg of you."

SUCH PATHOS was probably a rather alien concept for writer Heinrich Heine, who referred to himself as the last Romantic poet and had, as he saw it, "dealt the heaviest blows to the meaning of Romantic poetry in Germany." His poem "Epilogue" is also about last things, and cow herding plays a role in it as well. However, things here are decidedly this-worldly and robust in the best sense of the word:

> Graves they say are warm'd by glory
> Foolish words and empty story!
> Better far the warmth we prove
> From a cowgirl deep in love
> With her arms around us flung
> Reeking with the smell of dung.

In contrast to "Das Kchühorn" and the "Emmenthaler Kührei-hen," the cow here doesn't keep the lovers apart but is the link between them. She is only indirectly present through the fragrance of her excretions. But it's just that aroma that gives the imagined rendezvous with the milkmaid its special spice. For one thing, it makes the "foolish words" of the first line of the poem—the pathetic cliché that glory will outlive us and make even death more bearable—look particularly cold and stale.

The smell of cow dung might not seem particularly pleasant, let alone exciting. We have to remember, though, that that fragrance was a lot more popular in the nineteenth century than it is now. With hygiene in the cowsheds not being up to today's standards, the nourishing and sought-after cow products had an aroma that we would find rather strange. Even at the beginning of the twentieth century, dairy specialist trainees who took part in a blind taste test of milk deemed it tasty only when a pinch of cow dung had been mixed in. In the old days, the smell of bestial excrement was considered so beneficial that some sanatoriums had their own cowsheds in which ailing city dwellers could expose themselves to the healthy fragrances of country life in order to speed up recovery.

In fact, the fragrance may well have had a strong sexual appeal back then. During the winter people often slept with the animals to keep warm. They bedded themselves down next to the cows' plump and hefty bodies; children were fathered and born in their presence. Consciously or unconsciously the aroma of cow pies may have been linked to memories of the odd lovers' tryst next to warm, fragrant cow bodies.

Apart from the aphrodisiac smell of cow pies, the milkmaid also plays a considerable role in instigating intimacy: she is the one who takes the initiative "with her arms around us flung." So even Heinrich Heine was still caught up in the bucolic cliché of "simple" maids from the countryside who have qualities that the ladies from the cities lack: robust health and a refreshingly daring approach to matters of love. This concept is surprisingly consistent: Theocritus's young cowherd had already complained about the arrogant and cold-shouldered "city miss" who made a fuss about kissing and praised the comparative straightforwardness of women from the mountains. Some two millennia later, comic book series such as *Cowgirl Romances* propagated the sexual allure of the women by whom the West was won. And the sexual position in which the woman sits, as it were, "in the saddle," thus exercising greater control over her partner, is to this day referred to as "the cowgirl."

However, although the idea of the sexual recklessness of cowgirls prevailed into the twenty-first century, it had already been the subject of mockery for several hundred years. As early as 1714, the English satirical poet John Gay wrote a travesty of the bucolic genre entitled *The Shepherd's Week*, wherein he describes the hapless love of a milkmaid named Marian for a "swain" named Colin Clout. Although Marian's gentle hands "soft could stroke the udder'd cow," they could not stroke the skin of arrogant Colin. Depressed, she forgets about the dairy duties at which she used to excel: "But Marian now, devoid of country cares, / Nor yellow butter, nor sage-cheese prepares." Only at the very end of the poem, when Marian is comforted by the sight of a bull covering a cow, does she regain her appetite:

Thus Marian wail'd, her eyes with tears brimful,
When goody Dobbins brought her cow to bull:

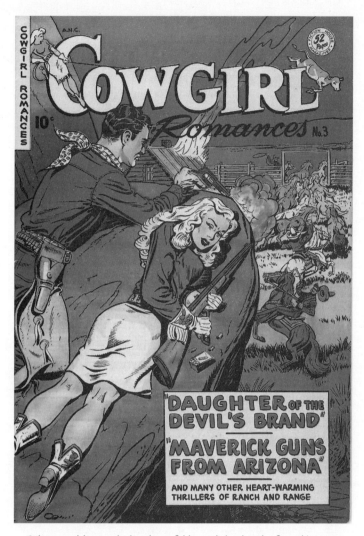

Sultry cowgirls were the heroines of this comic book series from the 1950s.

With apron blue to dry her tears she sought,
Then saw the cow well serv'd, and took a groat.


INDEED, ACCORDING to the great German humorist Wilhelm Busch, cows and poetry, be they bucolic or not, don't go together at all. In his story *Balduin Bählamm, der verhinderte Dichter* (Balduin Bählamm, the thwarted poet), Busch describes and illustrates the protagonist's increasingly desperate attempts to overcome his writer's block and finally fulfill his destiny by penning a poem. After three failed attempts, Bählamm believes he's found a solution: he has to leave the confines of his bourgeois urban environment; he must go to where the cows live—into nature.

So Bählamm leaves his wife and children and goes to the country, where he promptly finds the bucolic idyll he had in mind. A little boy is riding his hobbyhorse, "childlike and naively through a puddle." An older boy is standing next to his "cozy little dung heap." His eyes follow a girl who is busy cleaning the cowsheds and in the process, if we are to believe Heinrich Heine, acquiring a very special perfume. The circumstances for writing a poem seem ideal:

As soon as Bählamm there arrives,
Poetic genius revives.
The sun goes down, cowbells are ringing,
And set the poet's soul a-singing.
Thrilled by the natural extravaganza,
He has high hopes for his first stanza.

Unfortunately Bählamm has not figured in the cows. As long as they keep their distance and are only noticeable from afar as the sound of "cowbells ringing," they may well inspire the

A cow thwarts the poet Bählamm's work
in Wilhelm Busch's 1883 illustrated book.

poet. But when they suddenly become tangible and break into
the "reality" of the poet's chamber, the rural idyll comes to a
sudden end:

> Pots crash, he hears a heavy tread,
> Then there appears a horned head.
> Eyes closed, mouth wide. What does ensue?
> Crude country sounds, a loud *ra-moo!*

> Crushed by the noise are verse and rhyme,
> So is the poet's fine first line.
> Harsh sound will undo saint and sage.
> The bovine singer leaves the stage.

Cows seem to get in the way of the cowherd's leisure and the
bucolic poet's work. The very animal that enables bucolic
poetry in the first place puts its head through the window.

With a great roar it destroys all lyric composure and the metropolitan phantasm that the countryside is a particularly peaceful place conducive to poetic development.

Busch's story is in a way a "meta-bucolic" poem. It shows that it's difficult, maybe even impossible, to be among cows and to produce contemplative writings about them at the same time. However peaceful cows may seem, however much they epitomize calm and contentment, they are highly complex beings that can't easily be squeezed into poems, let alone a genre; and they are completely unsuited as mere extras for the lyric outpourings of out-of-touch city dwellers. As soon as we believe we are part of the happy country life, they break out of the role we have assigned to them and interrupt our dreams abruptly with a resounding and incomprehensible "Ra-moo!" Despite their eminent role in human culture, when it comes to such lofty matters as lovemaking or literature, cows are sometimes simply in the way.

# THE MOO

THAT COWS are able to produce very individualized utterances has been a known fact in German-speaking regions
at least since December 2007. That year, almost eleven
million viewers of the TV show *Wetten, dass...?* (Wanna bet
that...?) witnessed farmer Achim Jehle successfully identify
three of his dairy cows by the chomping and grinding noises
they made when eating an apple. Eighty-nine percent of the
viewers were thrilled by Ida's, Hilde's, and Luise's smacking
noises and the Swabian countryman's fine-tuned hearing,
and farmer Jehle became betting king. What took root in the
collective memory was not so much the sound of the chomping cows but the bizarre call with which the farmer called his
animals to their meal: "Mogii!"

In general, cows do express themselves vocally in much
more differentiated ways than one would assume. Cows welcome their newborn calves with a deep, persistent humming
sound to get them used to the frequency of the mother's voice.
When cows meet, they greet each other with a hearty bellow.

When they are hungry, they plaintively call for the farmer. And when they are in heat—a state that repeats itself about every three weeks and lasts for a maximum of two days—they fervently beg for a bull. "Their mooing becomes more strident, prolonged," French author Michel Houellebecq writes in his novel *Whatever*, "and its very harmonic texture modified to the point of recalling at times, and astonishingly so, certain groans which escape the sons of men." So it's not surprising that humans continue to conjecture that cows are really human beings who have been transformed and are trying to make themselves understood by mooing.

As Virgil tells us in the *Aeneid*, the cattle thief Cacus was forced to conclude that cows communicate vocally in unexpected ways. This "monster" stole four "splendid cows" and as many bulls from the hero Hercules, whose cattle were grazing in a valley on the Tiber. Cacus cunningly pulled the animals by their tails into a hideaway, reversing their hoofprints so that they wouldn't reveal their whereabouts. The fiend had, however, underestimated the cows' communication skills. The animals that had been left behind missed their companions and called out for the stolen cows when Hercules was about to herd them away.

> Preparing to be gone, the heifers, at parting, began to low, the whole grove was filled with their plaintive notes, and the hills with clamorous din were left. One of the heifers returned the sound, and pent up in the depth of the spacious cave re-bellowed, and frustrated the hopes of Cacus.

The answering call of the kidnapped cows tells Hercules where his cattle are. Enraged, he grabs his weapons, steals his frightened animals back, and strangles the fire-breathing Cacus.

In 1991, a group of Italian cattle thieves got off compara-tively lightly, when they were given nine months in prison for stealing fourteen head of cattle in the Lazio region. Here, too, the cows' plaintive calls were the thieves' downfall. When the owner entered the hideaway accompanied by the police, the cows immediately came running toward him, voicing their emotion very clearly. The farmer could thus without any doubt be identified as the rightful owner. "The cows immedi-ately recognized me and cried," he later said for the record. It would seem that, contrary to what Nietzsche believed, cows have a memory after all.

DESPITE THIS rather large spectrum of ways in which cows express themselves vocally (droning, bellowing, pleading, moaning, crying), we have only one onomatopoetic approxi-mation for the language of cows in English: moo. Cows don't fare any better in other languages, either. In German cows always say muh, in Spanish muuu, in French meuh, in Dutch boeh, in Norwegian bø, and in Hungarian bú. In practically all European languages, humans imitate the call of cows begin-ning with closed lips (an m or b sound), followed by a vowel that is also formed with an almost closed mouth, far back in the oral cavity. Only in Finnish do cows start their utterance with a short unrounded front vowel, saying ammuu.

The Italian philosopher Giorgio Agamben interprets the linguistic root *mu as a form of suppressed moan. It's the sound that a person produces when he wants to cry out in pain but can't for whatever reason, be it because he's gagged or is afraid of giving himself away by screaming. So in a sense, *mu represents the inability to communicate one's deeply felt suffering to the world. Hardly any other phonetic utterance comes closer to complete silence. Accordingly the Latin word for "silent" is mutus; it lives on in the English word mute. At the same time *mu is the etymological origin of the word mystery (mysterium in Latin). And, as Agamben puts it, at the heart of every mystery there's always a suffering, which "by its nature evades language." It corresponds to "something un-speakable, a closed-mouthed moaning." The mooing of cows is therefore, in the proper sense of the word, mysterious.

As we saw in the chapter on rumination, cows do indeed often have great difficulty expressing what they feel deep down. "They avoid expressing pain," writes veterinarian Melanie Feist, "because it's a sign of weakness that could have life-threatening consequences, if it were to attract the attention of a predator." The fact that our cattle moo is in fact a sign of domestication. In the wild, prey can never cry as loudly as in a pasture or a protected shed.

For a long time now, humans have interpreted the restrained phonetic utterances of cows as the epitome of mute suffering, as a symbol for the almost tragic inability to communicate with the world around them. Mahatma Gandhi counted cows among "God's mute creatures." Even in the fables of the Greek poet Aesop or the Baroque adaptations of Jean de la Fontaine, in which animals normally chat away for all they're worth, cows never have their say. They remain within the "world of the closed mouth," in Agamben's words. From a linguistic point of view, there's a certain logic to this. As Agamben notes, the word fable has its root in the Indo-Germanic *bha, which, unlike the syllable *mu, is formed with a wide-open mouth. It's hard to imagine a greater contrast to

the closed, mysterious mooing of cows. The linguistic limitations of cows become most obvious, however, in ancient
mythology: in the story of Io.

THE GIRL IO was one of the many rape victims of Jupiter, the
father of all gods (and the Roman equivalent of the Greek god
Zeus). As Ovid tells us in *Metamorphoses*, Io was so beautiful
that Jupiter was determined to exercise his *droit du seigneur* and
called her to a shady grove for a romp. He wanted to make
sure that his cow-eyed spouse Juno (the equivalent of the
Greek Hera) wouldn't be able to witness his adultery. When
Io ignored the god's instructions and fled from him, Jupiter
unceremoniously shrouded the world in cloud and took the
girl's "maidenhood" in the veil of mist.

Juno knew the usual tricks of her husband, who had frequently been caught in the act, all too well. She immediately
descended from the heavens and made the artificial fog disappear, whereupon Jupiter in his haste could think of nothing
better than to transform Io into a cow to conceal his infidelity.

> . . . She was still stunning.
> Even as a cow. Juno looked at her and couldn't help
> But admire her looks. Then she asked who she was,
> Where from, of what stock, as if she didn't know.
> Her husband, to forestall further inquiries, maintained
> That she was born of the earth, but Juno countered
> By demanding her as a gift. . .

The god doesn't dare refuse his wife's request, because "to
refuse so slight a gift as a cow to his sister and wife might
make the cow seem to be no cow at all," Ovid writes. In other

words, if Jupiter makes a big fuss about an alleged cow, his deceit might be uncovered. He reluctantly gives his transformed lover to his jealous spouse. She in turn gives the cow to Argus Panoptes (Argus "All-eyes") to watch over her. Argus lets her graze on the banks of the river where Io used to play as a child and where her family still lives.

The cruel thing about Io's situation isn't so much the unfamiliar food she has to eat ("leaves . . . and bitter herbs") or that she has to sleep on the hard ground. It is most of all the fact that she can no longer communicate with her "fellow humans" the way she used to.

> . . . When she would stretch
> Her suppliant arms to Argus, she had no arms to stretch,
> And when she tried to complain she only mooed.
> The sound startled her, and her own voice became a new
>     source of fear.

As with most metamorphoses, the transformation is only partial. Io has taken the shape of a cow but still has a human consciousness. Only her body, not her spirit, is affected by the metamorphosis, which is why Io perceives the few restricted sounds she can make with her cow mouth as so dreadful and frightening.

Io can't even communicate with her father or sisters when she encounters them on the river bank. Her relatives see nothing but a very beautiful cow who likes being petted by them, licks the palms of their hands, and occasionally moos (something the ancient Romans described with the onomatopoetic verb *mugire*). Only when Io draws her lamentable story into the soft sand of the river bank with her front hoof does her father understand the full scope of the tragedy.

Not only her father but also Io's ex-lover Jupiter can hardly bear the desperate groaning, sighing, and mooing. Jupiter dispatches his messenger Mercury, who first lulls Argus with his boring tales and then severs his head. But Io's salvation is still a long way away. To avenge the murder of her cowherd, Juno sends a blood-sucking insect, a vicious little fury that chases Io all around the globe: "Aha! Aha! Poor me!" the plagued cow cries in the play *Prometheus Bound* by the tragedian Aeschylus. "Again the gadfly stings me, miserable roamer." For dramaturgic reasons, Io has the power of speech this once. According to stage directions, the actor playing Io has to appear wearing horns as a sign that the character's been transformed into a cow.

While trying to escape to Asia Minor, Io traverses a strait—since then named Bosporus ("cow strait") in her honor—and eventually reaches the region around what is now Egypt. This is where Io is finally released after Jupiter has sworn to his wife to keep clear of her.

> As the goddess calms down, Io regains
> Her previous form and becomes what she was.
> The bristles recede, the horns decrease, the great eyes
> Grow smaller, the jaws contract, arms and hands
> Return, and each solid hoof becomes five nails again.

Stories that offer explanations for natural or psychological phenomena are a hallmark of *Metamorphoses*. The lovesick Echo burns with self-destructive love and disintegrates into nothing—which explains the phenomenon of the echo. The boy Hyacinthus suffers a deadly head wound while discus throwing—which is why the flowers named after him have drooping heads. The girl Io dreads speaking because she's afraid that a pitiful moo rather than her intended, well-formed words will come out of her mouth—symbolic of the occasional human dilemma of *wanting* to say much more than we *can*.

How often are we trying to unburden our heart to a loved one or to give someone we detest a piece of our mind, only to find ourselves simply unable to put into words the things that cause so much turmoil in our heart, stomach, or gall bladder? How often do we, as the Gospel of Matthew puts it, feel an "abundance of the heart" but our mouth just won't speak? Instead of words gushing out of us, nothing but a puny linguistic trickle leaves our lips, as if the mouth were a funnel allowing but a fraction of what goes on inside to escape. Although most of us are presumably able to produce more sophisticated utterances than Io as a cow, there's always an asymmetry between our thoughts and feelings on the one hand and what we say on the other. And we have no control over how our words are perceived by the person to whom they are directed: as a suppressed plea for help, as "a closed-mouthed moaning," as Agamben puts it, or just as a muffled, stupid moo. The story of Io, as told by Ovid, is ultimately about the tragedy of human communication.

COMPARABLE MYTHS from other epochs and parts of the world point to the fact that this experience is general to all humans and not confined to antiquity or Greco-Roman culture. The male first-person narrator in the novel *My Life in the Bush of Ghosts* by Nigerian writer Amos Tutuola goes through an experience similar to Io's. Tutuola's narrative style is strongly anchored in oral traditions and at times sounds awkward, even "wrong," to Western ears. The fantastic, almost hallucinogenic, pictorial quality of his writing essentially relates to the folklore of the Nigerian Yoruba. And yet, certain parallels with Ovid's *Metamorphoses* are obvious.

The hero and narrator of Tutuola's novel is a seven-year-old boy. He has to leave his village after it has been attacked by enemy warriors. On the run from his persecutors, he gets lost in the "bush of ghosts." There, in the heart of the jungle, he encounters a series of supernatural characters, each one more terrifying than the last. One of the most repulsive ones is the so-called Smelling-Ghost, a giant, foul-smelling creature that is covered in insects, wears scorpions on its fingers as rings, and belts his trousers with a live boa constrictor. The Smelling-Ghost wants to transform the boy into a horse and use it to ride to a meeting of ghosts. But the boy manages to escape: he steals the ghost's magic talisman, thus transforming himself into a cow.

Although he can now outrun the ghost, he also seems to have jumped out of the frying pan and into the fire. First he encounters a hungry lion that wants him for lunch. Then he's captured by cowherds who mistake him for one of their animals that has run away and so punish him severely. Like Io, the transformed cow-boy suffers from having to eat unfamiliar food. But most of all he, like the Greek girl, suffers from being unable to communicate with the cowherds.

> I was unable to explain to these cow-men that I was not really a cow, so that I was showing them in my attitude several times that I am a person because whenever they were roasting yams in the fire and when eating it I would approach them and start to eat the crumbs of the yams that were falling down by mistake from their hands and

whenever they were discussing some important matter with arguments within themselves I would be giving
signs with my head which was showing them the right
and wrong points on which they were arguing.

Unfortunately the cowherds don't understand his sign language. They think the cow is stubborn and beat her. And
when the animal still refuses to eat grass, they sell her to
an old woman who wants to sacrifice the cow to the village
ghosts, hoping that will cure her daughter's blindness. The
protagonist's life is threatened again: he is taken to the sacrificial altar by a crowd armed with bush knives, spears, and
axes. And again, words fail him when he wants to reveal
himself:

> At this stage I wanted to speak to them that I am not a real
> cow but a person. But all this was in vain, because if my
> heart speaks as a person my mouth would speak out the
> words in the cow's voice which was fearful to them and
> also was not clear to them.

Luckily the villagers' minds are already on the feast of beef
that will follow the sacrifice, and the boy manages to escape
the distracted crowd. He runs back into the bush of ghosts,
where he falls into a pond formed during the rainy season. He
sees his reflection in the water's surface, and to his surprise
he's been transformed back into a human being.

So the chapter "My Life with Cows" is not just about
the challenge of linguistic communication but also about
another sensory limitation: muteness is joined by blindness.
This comes up explicitly with the daughter whose blindness the cow sacrifice is supposed to cure. But figuratively

speaking, it also touches all other characters in this episode. The Smelling-Ghost doesn't notice that his talisman is stolen. The cowherds ignore the sign language the boy is using to try to communicate. And last but not least, the hero himself is struck with blindness. Only when he finally sees his own reflection, when he becomes aware of his "true nature," can he become human again; only through self-awareness can he gain freedom.

This story, fantastic as it may seem, does have a real political background. Amos Tutuola was from West Africa, the region that was most affected by transatlantic human trafficking. When his novel was published in 1954, Nigeria was still under British rule. So it's hardly surprising that slavery is, more or less explicitly, one of the central themes of *My Life in the Bush of Ghosts*. The armed men who raid the protagonist's village are obviously human traffickers. The master-servant relationship is also a recurring theme in the mythical sphere of the bush of ghosts. When the protagonist meets the first ghostly figures, they already argue about which of them will be allowed to keep him as a slave. The snake-belted Smelling-Ghost wants to turn him into his mount. And the cowherds, into whose hands he finally falls, treat and sell him on with the same indifference they would show toward a cow, or a serf, whom they can beat and sell on as they see fit. Only the look into the water's reflective surface ends this phase of slavery.

In the eyes of his owners, the boy in Tutuola's novel is but a cow. In order to meet the expectations of the cowherds, he could simply adhere to his role, behave like a cow, and eat grass. Instead he distances himself from his "fellow creatures" and imitates the cowherds' behavior. And yet, like those Afro-American slaves who tried to emulate their "masters'" behavior and donned a suit and top hat on Sundays, he is not accepted as an equal, as a human being. He may well eat yams and try to join in the conversation, but they still regard him as a cow, or even worse, as a stubborn, presumptuous cow. Only when he has escaped his owners' sway and catches the first literally unprejudiced glimpse of himself is he transformed from an "object" into an autonomous being. He promptly regains the gift of speech and, suddenly self-conscious, goes on to trick his pursuers:

> But as I had been changed into a person before these people came with guns, I asked them personally what they were looking for, but they replied that they were looking for a cow which was just escaped from them, then I said—"Oh! I saw it now when running far into the bush, better follow this way, you will see it very soon if you follow my advice."

By letting his protagonist temporarily slip into a cow's hide, Amos Tutuola, like the poet Ovid two thousand years before him, gave us direct insight into the life and thought of cows. According to the two authors, the most excruciating shortcoming of these animals is their, at least to human ears, severely limited vocabulary. Whatever cows try to tell us, all we understand is "moo."

And Ovid and Tutuola also draw our attention to another trait of cows: they're usually the captives of humans. Few other animal species have let themselves be domesticated so willingly, and no other is kept in larger numbers. So it's not surprising that the state of affairs of cows has again and again been metaphorically identified with that of prisoners, employees, or slaves—and it's this relationship between cows and freedom that we'll look at next.

# BEHIND THE FENCE

A HERD OF black-and-white cows, crowded together in the cowshed as dusk falls; the milky light of spring filtering through the window. The cows are snorting, flapping their ears: there's an air of unrest in the shed. Suddenly the door opens as if by magic. The cows step out, at first still hesitatingly, dodging their heads like the blinded pilgrims in Plato's "Allegory of the Cave." But then they become more impetuous. They, in the words of Beat Sterchi, quickly get "over the stupor of being kept shut in all winter" and frolic on the pasture. They romp across the fresh grass, virtually hop, skip, and jump, and quite obviously enjoy their newly gained freedom to the fullest—until they come to a sudden stop in front of an electric fence. The distinctive, regular clicking of the electric fence controller is audible. One of the cows inspects the square box with her mouth and then moos reproachfully. Cut—we see her from behind. The cow is standing on the coast and seems to be staring longingly out to sea.

In the short film *Schwarzbunt Märchen* (Black-pied fairytale), one of the first works of German filmmaker Detlev

Buck, there are no human actors at all; according to the credits, it was made with hardly any human cooperation. In Detlev Buck's typically dry manner, the credits read: "Director: probably Distel oder Imke"—German names for cows. However, the film addresses one of the essential aspects of the human-cow relationship: cows are our prisoners. Even if they are among the happy cows that don't have to spend their whole lives in the cowshed but are allowed out into the pasture in the summer, their freedom is clearly limited—for example, by electric fences. And even if they are able to overcome the limits that humans impose, there are always other obstacles ahead. In this case it's the sea, which can be interpreted as a symbol for the endpoint of accessible space or—as infinite and unfathomable as it seems to the cow's eye—for the end of a lifespan. And that limit is usually also imposed by humans.

ONE OF the most bewildering characteristics of cows is that, despite their size and strength, and although they're equipped with a quite substantial weapon in the form of horns, they endure their bondage mostly without complaint or resistance. In 1925, poet Bertolt Brecht, ever a stalwart ally of the damned of this earth, wrote the poem "Cow at Cud." It exemplifies empathetically the contentment and forbearance with which domestic cattle accept their life in the service of humans:

> Against the brye rail her dewlap strains.
> She feeds on bales of hay, but is polite:
> chews thirty times at least every bite,
> extracts each drop from straw that splits the veins.
>
> Her hardened haunch and rheumy eyes are old:
> so much behind her, nothing to but cud:

the years have cooled the ardour of her blood.
She's not surprised by anything, I'm told.

And when she works her chops somebody draws
with sweaty hands thick, flyblown milk from her;
it could be clothes-pegs pinching on her udder,

she isn't bothered by the farmyard raws.
What's going on is neither here nor there.
So, dropping dung, she takes the evening air.

The fact that the poem is written as a sonnet, the preferred form for wistful love poetry since the Renaissance, points to the narrator's affection for the oppressed creature. In Petrarch or Shakespeare an unattainable lover usually takes the place of the cow. There is, however, a note of resignation in Brecht's description of the beloved cow. Her aversion against "evil" and her exploitation by humans are reflected only in the animal's body language and facial expression (the sadness in her eyes and the disdainful raising of her weary brow) but not in her deeds. And the only action that could be interpreted as a sign of passive resistance—that is, the dropping of a cow pie during milking, is attributed to the auspicious "evening air." Such devoted animals are unlikely to bring about a revolution. Even on their way to the slaughterhouse cows tend to keep their countenance and resign themselves to their fate, as Beat Sterchi describes in his novel *The Cow*:

> Immune to scorn, Blösch declined to lower her head and butt, made no use of the strength that still dwelt in her great body. Even given the justification of self-defense, she still declined to use any kind of force. She

was civilized inside and out, horn to udder, and even on
the abattoir platform she remained submissive and meek.
These principles had worldwide currency, and Blösch
stayed true to them to the last.

With this, Sterchi gives an important hint as to why cows
don't rebel against their fate even when faced with impending
death. In animals as big and strong as cows, submissiveness
and meekness are understandably desirable selection criteria.
Fierceness and the will to resist have been bred out of them as
far as possible during thousands of years of captivity.

At the same time, and this may sound paradoxical, cows
also benefit from their enslavement by humans. It was only
by letting themselves be domesticated by humans that they
could rise to be the most widespread and numerous large
mammal on earth. They paid the price of freedom for a symbiotic relationship with humans and were thus protected from
the dangers and burdens of life in the wild.

Veterinarian and cow specialist Michael Brackmann views
it as an "ingenious gambit" from the point of view of biological selection that the Eurasian urus, the aurochs, adapted to
humans. By leaving it to humans to provide food and shel-
ter, it could concentrate exclusively on the essentials of the
species's survival: "the passing on and propagation of genes;
reproduction." With this, Brackmann contradicts the popular
notion that romanticizes nature and that labels our domestic cattle as particularly stupid and wild animals as especially
smart. On the contrary, he reckons, the latter were just not
clever enough to get themselves domesticated—"of course
only from a socio-biological point of view."

This, of course, doesn't mean that domesticated cattle
will always behave particularly smart in the short or medium

run. There's an ultimate and very mundane reason why cows dutifully endure their imprisonment, why they usually spare humans who cross their pasture, and why a ramshackle barbed-wire fence or a few milliseconds of electric shock from an electric fence keep them from trying to escape: they're just not aware of their truly superhuman strength.

Animal psychologist Temple Grandin confirms this opinion. She writes: "The fences farmers use only work to keep cattle in because the cattle don't realize that they have the power to break through them." If they occasionally manage to open the latch of a fence, it's more likely due to chance and their proclivity to repeatedly lick objects. Collective breakaways of cows probably manifest themselves most dramatically in so-called stampedes, which in the case of huge Wild West herds could sometimes cost casual bystanders and cowboys their lives. However, such breakaways are not deliberate acts of resistance but panic reactions. In Elias Canetti's words, the cows form a "flight crowd," which is "created by a threat . . . [They] flee together because it is best to flee that way . . . The crowd has, as it were, become all direction, away from danger."

THIS IS one of the fundamental differences between humans (on whom Canetti's writing really focuses) and cattle: with the exception of seeing a few especially juicy blades of grass on the other side of the fence, the cow can't visualize what lies beyond the restricted living space allotted to her and so can't imagine a utopia that could induce her to break free from her imprisonment. Sociologically speaking, she reacts to push rather than pull factors. As part of the fleeing crowd, she strains to get away from a perceived immediate danger—but she never moves toward a future that she imagines to be better.

And yet, cows have always been used as a benchmark for repressive interpersonal relationships, for forms of slavery, serfdom, or wage-dependent relations. It's no coincidence that we talk about "a yoke around the neck" in connection with cattle as well as with humans when their bodies and strength are usurped. As early as the seventeenth century, the English political theorist James Harrington commented that Scottish people were "little better than the cattle of the nobility." And in the nineteenth century, one observer complained that at hiring-fairs, men and women stood "in droves, like cattle, for inspection." Bertolt Brecht also highlights the human-cattle parallel very explicitly in his teaching play *Saint Joan of the Stockyards*. The play shows how the employees of Chicago's slaughterhouses and meat factories are plunged into poverty by their employers' gambling on the stock market. Although the workers aren't slaughtered in the actual sense of the word, they are, in every other respect, treated as arbitrarily as those animals that they process to produce canned meat. While waiting in vain for the start of their shift in front of the meat factory that has been closed owing to speculative trading, they compare themselves to cattle: "What do they take us for? Do they think we'll stand around like steers, ready for anything?" The factory managers who let the starving proletariat, whom they have forced into unemployment, slowly bleed to death are later reviled as "human butchers" by the workers. "For it happens alike with Man and Beast," it says in Alfred Döblin's novel *Berlin Alexanderplatz*, which was written at the same time and takes place in a similar setting. "As the Beast dies, so Man dies, too."

Even more serious than the metaphorical equation *humans = cattle* is the accusation that humans are not just treated "like cattle" but worse. In his 1798 *Schilderung der Gebirgsvölker der Schweitz* (Portrait of the mountain peoples of Switzerland), travel writer Johann Gottfried Ebel vents his outrage at the fact that the peasantry in large areas of Europe was still subject to bondage or hereditary serfdom:

> In the Appenzell region cows are treated with more of the kind of respect that is due every useful natural being and are happier than millions of people in Europe, who curse their lives of suppression and hardship. Is it possible that at the end of the eighteenth, the so-called philosophical century, this parallel is a reality, one of such truly scandalous proportions?—Hideous reality!!

Over the following decades the liberation of the peasantry led to a gradual repeal of the manorial system that Ebel deplores here. But in many cases new dependencies took its place, especially with the advancement of industrialization and the development of a large urban working class; and as the example of Brecht's *Saint Joan of the Stockyards* shows, the circumstances of this new wage-dependent class were often either equated with those of cattle or exemplified with cows. In Alfred Döblin's *Berlin Alexanderplatz*, too, the fall of its protagonist is mirrored in the description of a slaughterhouse scene. Like the bull that's stunned by the butcher's huge hammer and whose killing is described in detail in book four of the novel, Franz Bieberkopf suffers one blow after the next, until he lands way down, at the very bottom rung of society. Similarly, in Walter Ruttmann's 1927 documentary *Berlin: Symphony of a Metropolis*, we see a quick sequence of images of workers and cows rushing toward the factory and the slaughterhouse, respectively. It almost seems as if the cows have joined the farmers in the industrial revolution and have come to the city to find a new home, becoming the leading metaphor for the circumstances of the workers there.

This parallel highlights various aspects that are responsible for the spate of cow metaphors in the age of industrialization. For one thing, cows, like factory workers in early capitalism, normally appear in "herds"—that is, their owners or employers see them as a faceless crowd rather than a collection of individuals. Secondly, it's mostly others who benefit from their labor: what they generate is either literally or virtually "milked." Furthermore, cows and workers both carry out monotonous physical activities at the behest of others, be it at the feeding trough or on the assembly line. And yet, they are expected to not complain, moo, or protest in any other form.

A poster designed by French painter Henri de Toulouse-Lautrec for the magazine La Vache Enragée in 1896 illustrates the political point of view of cows and workers and of the artists who depict them. In it, the "raging cow" who gave the magazine its name chases a desperate older gentleman through the streets of Paris. The policeman in pursuit tries in vain to catch her. Three passers-by observe the whole scene with some amusement. The fleeing gentleman's portly figure, his frock coat, and fine collarless shirt with its frilly sleeves mark him as a member of the bourgeoisie. The cow's coat reveals her political colors: red is, after all, not only the color of rage but also that of socialism. The issue of La Vache Enragée was indeed published on the occasion of a carnival-like parade that was organized by Parisian partisan artists as a counter-event to the traditional Fête du Boeuf Gras celebrations and held the day before Ash Wednesday. Instead of honoring "fat beef" as a sign of opulence, the Bohemians celebrated the

Henri de Toulouse-Lautrec's poster for the magazine *La Vache Enragée* (1896).

"enraged cow" as a symbol of the paucity that prevailed among the impoverished inhabitants of Montmartre. At the time, the expression *manger la vache enragée*, "to eat the enraged cow," was commonly used in socialist and anarchic circles to paraphrase hunger.

However, it was probably the Russian director Sergei Eisenstein who most impressively equated the destiny of the proletariat with that of cows. He used a cinematic technique of his own invention: the montage. In this technique, independently occurring and causally unrelated dramatic actions are associatively linked to each other by film editing. Eisenstein's first feature-length film, *Strike*, was shot in 1925 but is set during the 1917 October Revolution in czarist Russia. Undignified working conditions and the suicide of a colleague have led to an organized walkout in an unidentified factory. (Pre-revolutionary strikes in Yaroslavl, Tsaritsyn, and other cities in Russia's industrial central region served as historical models for the film.) The factory management first tries to handle the situation by using undercover informants. When that fails and the workers' demands become more and more exigent, the management has the strikers massacred. The displayed intertitle succinctly reads "Slaughter." And that's exactly what the audience gets to see next: images of workers who are brutally murdered by soldiers on horseback in an open field. Then, inserted by abrupt cuts, follow camera shots from a slaughterhouse, the archetypal location of indifferent serial killings. A cow is stunned with a bolt between her eyes. She collapses, her legs still flailing as she lies there, as if she is trying to escape her destiny, but it's all in vain: the butcher holds her firmly and cuts her main artery with a knife. Black blood gushes from her throat, she rolls her eyes as if looking for its source—then a last (cinematic) cut and we see a battlefield of murdered female and male workers.

In the course of the twentieth century, people were indeed treated like animals, and not just in the metaphorical sense. In some cases animal husbandry practices were directly applied to humans. This started with the Russo-Japanese war but became prevalent during the trench warfare of World War I. It was during that period that barbed wire, invented by American farmer Joseph F. Glidden in 1870, was used for warfare on a large scale. It served to mount lines of defense. The first electric fences were also erected during that time. Charged with a deadly high voltage, they separated German-occupied Belgium from the Netherlands. It was, however, the Nazis who applied animal husbandry practices most relentlessly to humans. Not only were the concentration camps of the Third Reich surrounded by barbed wire and electric fences; according to author Thomas Kapielski, their entire conception was modeled on the cowshed. "As far as the management style, topology, architecture, structures, etc., of these giant cowsheds are concerned," he writes, "they are—whether consciously or unconsciously—a structural and genealogical matrix for a concentration camp."

But the inhuman treatment of those who were locked up and murdered in the death camps began much earlier. "The dehumanizing began the moment we climbed into those cattle cars," is how Holocaust survivor Zwi Bacharach remembers the transport to Auschwitz-Birkenau. "We were treated like cattle." Accordingly, the metaphor of animal husbandry and killing was applied to the Nazi murderers. Camp physician Aribert Heim, who conducted cruel and often deadly experiments on prisoners, is often called "the butcher of Mauthausen." Gestapo chief Klaus Barbie, responsible for torturing and murdering Jews and resistance members in occupied France, is referred to as "the butcher of Lyon"; and Governor General Hans Frank, who ruled in Krakow, is called "the butcher of Poland."

The word "butcher" is meant to emphasize the extraordinary indifference and brutality with which these men killed or tortured their victims. But it doesn't do justice to the magnitude of the crime. After all, a butcher treats the cows at his mercy more humanely than the Nazi perpetrators treated their victims. And even cows kept in giant cowsheds, no matter how structurally similar these buildings may be to Nazi concentration camps, are still "treated as property, and therefore better"—that is, "like slaves," in the words of Thomas Kapielski. The latter may be physically unfree, but their owners normally have enough self-interest not to harm them.

Jewish philosopher Vilém Flusser, who in 1940 had to flee his native Prague to escape the Nazis, used the image of cow husbandry to express much more subtle forms of bondage and suppression. Flusser sees cows as "a danger and a threat" mostly because human development might, little by little, follow that of cows, and because humans might themselves, without noticing it, become prisoners—in essence, cows.

To Flusser, the cow is a "machine," even the very "prototype for the ultimate future machine" that is "designed with ecologically developed technology. We can indeed already claim that the cow is the triumph of a future-oriented technology." She changes grass into milk. She reproduces automatically. She's an "authentic open work," a sort of "open source" document incarnate that's constantly changed by cross-breeding and can be adjusted to the respective local conditions (mountains, pastures, steppe). And when the cow-machine finally starts showing age-related signs of wear and tear, "its 'hardware' can be used in the form of meat, leather, and other consumable products."

This idea may leave the utilitarian minded largely indifferent. They might even welcome it, were it not, as Flusser notes, for their inclination to imitate machines. From steam engines in the eighteenth century, to the chemical factories of the nineteenth, to the computers and digital networks of the late-twentieth and early-twenty-first centuries, people have always and still do model their thoughts and actions on the latest technical achievements. And according to Flusser, that's where the danger lies. "The slow substitution of modern machines by machines of the cow kind can lead to an identification of people with cows: human = cow." As long as humans are surrounded by more than a billion cows, as long as they live in the constant presence of cow products in the form of cheese, milk, leather, and beef and the remains of decommissioned cow-machines, they can't escape the cows' influence. "The very presence of the cow has a cow-like influence. Our mind refuses to imagine the consequences."

Defying all resistance, Flusser subsequently creates a scenario that shows the result of the triumphant cow-machines and could well be part of a dark science-fiction movie like *The Matrix* or *The Island* (which didn't hit screens until years after Flusser's death). In *The Matrix*, humankind has been enslaved and is kept as an energy source by an artificial intelligence that maintains world domination. In *The Island*, a society of clones is led to believe that at the end of their working life they'll be rewarded with a dream journey to an island paradise. In reality their journey takes them straight to the slaughterhouse as organ donors: they are used as live spare-part depots. In Flusser's dystopian futuristic vision, humankind has turned into "a herd of cows":

> A grazing and ruminating, content and unselfconscious human race who will consume grass, who will produce milk for an invisible elite of "cowherds" who are

interested in it. This kind of human race will be manip-
ulated so gently and cleverly that it will think itself
free . . . Life will be restricted to typically bovine functions: birth, consumption, rumination, production,
leisure, reproduction, death. A heavenly yet frightening
prospect. When we behold the cow, do we not see tomor-
row's humanity?

There are two aspects that turn people into cow-machines in
those kinds of films—and if we are to believe Flusser, some-
day this might happen in the "real world" too. Firstly, people's
intelligence is kept artificially limited so that they can't revolt
against their "owners." Like cows, they know nothing about
the world beyond their cognitive gates. Secondly, this kind of
intellectual limitation is primarily designed so that the rulers
can use people not in their role as "working animals" but as a
tangible resource to be harvested.

In a sense, the parasitic use of human beings, of their bodies and fluids, is already happening. What's presented as a
sci-fi vision is really nothing but a distillation and exaggeration of existing tendencies. Already centuries ago, women,
mostly from the lower social classes, made their milk available to a very visible elite of "cowherds." By working as wet
nurses, they relieved the ladies of the nobility and the bourgeoisie from the burdens of nursing. Today, in the twenty-first
century, which despite its tender age is already referred to as
the "century of the life sciences," access to the female (and
less so the male) body is much more far reaching. The use
of the human as resource is focused on Flusser's themes of
"birth," "production," and "reproduction."

As surrogate mothers women carry the children of other
parents to full term. Men donate sperm to allow other

couples to become pregnant. At the embryonic stage children are selected based on their genetic make-up so that, if necessary, they will later on be able to act as a "savior sibling" for their sick brother or sister by donating bone marrow. All of these procedures reduce the human being, at least temporarily, to his or her function as a harvestable resource. He or she is a milk-producing animal, a uterus, a stock bull, the sum of a set of desirable genetic characteristics. And all of these procedures have been used in a similar way for years in cattle breeding.

Contemporary human beings have an affinity toward Flusser's other "typical functions of the cow," a fact that can't be overlooked. The buzzwords "consumption, rumination, . . . leisure" certainly dominate the modern media and wellness society. There's a certain appeal in the bovine blueprint for life that revolves around a happily ruminating existence. Who doesn't indulge in a simple work-leisure-consumption routine from time to time, eschewing, as Friedrich Nietzsche writes with respect to cows, "all grave thoughts which bloat the heart"? Who wouldn't like to believe that we make our decisions independently, free from the manipulations of the media, art, or advertising? Even Flusser has to admit that there's something desirable about such a dependent but carefree life.

However, he believes that we shouldn't give in to the gradual "bovinization" of humanity without a fight. "The progress toward the cow can still be stopped." Not by "denying the obvious advantages of cows and the creative imagination that is revealed through them, but by trying to adapt the cow . . . to true human ideals." In other words, if for centuries humans have been compared to cows, if at times they treat their fellow humans like cows, if they themselves should one day turn into some type of cow, then it's high time to treat cows like humans. Or better yet, to treat them the way humans would ideally be treated. And if living in freedom is a human ideal, then humans will have to free the cows who have been their prisoners for thousands of years.

# SACRED COWS

SOME YEARS ago a train derailed in the Khagaria district in Northeast India, near the Nepalese border. The conductor made an emergency stop while the train was going at full speed. Several of the overcrowded carriages subsequently plunged off a bridge. More than 240 people died. The reason for the disaster: a cow was standing on the tracks. The conductor wanted to avoid hitting her at all cost.

For Western observers such behavior is very hard to understand. That cows are considered sacred in India may be one of the most widely spread clichés about the subcontinent. The fact that the animals are allowed to stand around wherever they please without being hassled, while the traffic flows around them like water around a rock, is viewed with a sort of condescending admiration. What a strange country where people show half-starved cattle such respect. And aren't there even retirement homes for cows who can no longer feed themselves? And yet, probably nobody in the West would think of jeopardizing the lives of countless people for the sake of a cow. In English the expression "sacred cow" is at best used metaphorically and normally refers to something that can't be tampered with, for fear of public outcry; it's been used to describe anything from agricultural subsidies to low tuition fees to employment insurance. If someone in a Western cultural context claims that something is a sacred cow, there's an underlying subtext: the animal should be slaughtered.

IN INDIA, on the other hand, home to one sixth of the world's population and one tenth of its cows, the slaughtering of cattle is prohibited in most states; according to Brahmin teaching it's even considered murder. A person who kills a cow is said go through dozens of transmigrations before dropping to the lowest level of incarnation. Even someone who kills a cow by accident—as would have happened to the unfortunate conductor, had he not managed to derail the train in time—is guilty. He must shave his head and go to a cow pasture. There he has to wrap himself in the hide of the killed animal and for one month swallow the dust raised by the cows. Until the early 1970s, killing a cow could incur the death penalty in Kashmir. At first sight, this may seem excessive, but considering that according to Hindu belief 330 million gods and goddesses are inherent in every cow, such harsh punishment may be more understandable.

For Hindus the cow is the mother of all life and, in the words of Mahatma Gandhi, "the embodiment of the whole infra-human world" and "a poem of compassion." Cows are omnipresent in the Vedas, the oldest holy books of Hinduism. There they are compared, among other things, to the mother of the heavenly gods, to the earth, to the cosmic waters, to motherliness, and to the art of poetry. According to mythology, Krishna, one of the most popular Hindu deities, grew up among cowherds and so is also known by the epithet *Govinda*, "the cow-finder," and is often depicted with a zebu by his side. Many of the religious Hindu customs would be inconceivable without various cow products. Temple statues are rinsed daily with cow's milk. The lamps that hang in temples are fuelled with ghee, clarified butter made from cow's milk. Sick children are bathed in cow urine, which is considered a sacred liquid. During festivals, priests knead Krishna figurines from cow dung.

Why cows of all things have gained such importance in India is a matter of some controversy. Gandhi always emphasized the spiritual, altruistic dimension of Indian cow worship. But he also admitted that there are tangible economic explanations. "Why the cow was selected for apotheosis is obvious to me . . . The cow was—in India—the best companion. She was the giver of plenty. Not only did she give milk, she also made agriculture possible." The (linguistically idiosyncratic) essay "The Cow" by an Indian civil servant, passed down by American writer Paul Bowles, points in a similar direction. (Bowles was touched to learn that the civil servant had written the text in order to prove his foreign language skills.)

> The cow is one wonderful animal . . . He is same like God, sacred to Hindu and useful to man . . . His whole body can be utilized for use. More so the milk. What it cannot do? Various ghee, butter, cream, curds, whey, kova and the condensed milk and so forth. Also, he is useful to cobbler, watermans and mankind generally. His motion is slow only. That is because he is of amplitudinous

species, and also his other motion is much useful to trees, plants as well as making fires. This is done by making flat cakes in hand and drying in the sun.

This last, somewhat vague point is of particular importance. The "other motion" of cows, their bowel function, not only provides Hindu priests with the raw material for Krishna figurines; it's also the basis of the Indian energy industry and of its fertilizer industry. Indian cows produce approximately 700 million tons of usable dung per year. About half of it is used for agricultural fertilization, and the other half is dried and used as fuel. The metabolism of cows provides more than half of the energy consumed by Indian households. The yearly heating value of burned-up cow pies is equivalent to 85 million tons of wood or 64 million tons of coal.

In rural India, where many smallholders can't afford motorized machinery, cattle are also important draft animals and play a vital role in animal-drawn transport. As such they enable agriculture, as Gandhi said. The cow is therefore not primarily a provider of dairy or meat but a four-legged tractor and "the factory that produces the ox," as the ethnologist Marvin Harris puts it. Harris argues that the deification of the Indian cow and the associated taboo against eating beef are rooted in the animal's use as agricultural machinery. They prevent Indian farmers from slaughtering their tractors and tractor factories during the regularly occurring droughts. The seemingly irrational cow worship may have meant short- or medium-term periods of famine, but it ensured long-term survival.

Last but not least, the worship of sacred cows on the Indian subcontinent also has political significance. Eschewing beef has allowed Hindus to differentiate themselves from "cow-murdering Muslims," (in the words of Clemens Six), and to thereby reinforce their own identity.

But the food taboo against cows was by no means established with the beginning of Hinduism. According to Indian historian D.N. Jha it wasn't until the early Middle Ages that the slaughter and consumption of cows began to be considered taboo. With the emergence of the nationalistic cow protection movement at the end of the nineteenth century, the cow finally became a tool of mass political mobilization. The slaughter of cows was now interpreted as an attack on Hinduism per se. Prior to the division of British India into the Republic of India and the Islamic Republic of Pakistan, the cow protection movement repeatedly led to bloody riots. Apparently even the worship of an animal as peaceable as the cow doesn't necessarily mean renouncing violence.

HINDUISM IS probably the best-known religion to worship the cow as a divine being. It is, however, by no means the first or only one. Sumerians already worshipped the deity Ninlil, a goddess in the shape of a cow. The Mesopotamians believed that whenever she lay with her god husband, Enlil, the Bull of Heaven, the Euphrates and Tigris rivers would burst their banks and flood the land, thus making it fertile.

The ancient Egyptians similarly believed that the heavens above were really the womb of a gigantic divine cow. Her head was thought to be as broad as the valley of the Nile; the coat of her underbelly showed the firmament with its stars—that's how she's depicted in pharaoh Tutankhamen's outer shrine, for example. Since the heavenly cow supposedly emerged from the primordial waters, still carrying her life-giving

An illustration of the divine cow that appears on
Tutankhamen's outermost shrine.

origins within her as a milk donor, she was often referred to
as Mehet-Weret—"Great Flood" or "Great Swimmer." She was
also often equated to or intermixed with other mother goddesses, mostly with Isis and the goddess Hathor, who is also
depicted as a cow, a woman with a cow's head, or at least one
with cow's horns. As she was considered to be the mother of
sun god Ra, pictures show her carrying him on her back or as
a sun disk between her horns.

The Fulbe, a pastoral tribe living in the Sahelian zone,
believe that God created the world from a drop of milk that
came from the udder of the divine cow Itoori. The Guinean
author Tierno Monénembo (who is an ethnic Fulbe) recounts
the act of creation as follows: "Geno, the eternal, first created
the cow. Then he created woman. And only then the Fulbe.
He placed the woman behind the cow. He placed the Fulbe
behind the woman."

There are reports of a divine cow not only in Asian and African but also Germanic mythology. According to the Prose Edda in Old Norse, a cow named Auðumbla emerged from the ice at the beginning of creation. She nourished the giant Ymir, who was still caught in the glacier, with her streams of milk. With her warm tongue she then thawed a human whose grandson would later on kill Ymir and seize power over heaven and earth. "She licked the blocks of ice, which were salty . . . and as she licked these stones of ice rime, the hair of a man appeared in the blocks toward the evening. On the second came the man's head, and on the third day, the whole man."

Despite all their cultural and theological differences, these figures have something in common. They all are remarkably peaceable gods—to be otherwise would indeed be surprising for creatures that appear as cows. They normally watched over agricultural societies whose way of life made them dependent on political and climatic continuity and who tended, in contrast to nomadic peoples, to be averse to conflict. "The gods of the herdsmen guaranteed military victory and booty," writes Jeremy Rifkin, "the gods of the cultivators guaranteed the spring flood and fall harvests. [They] were more sedentary and predictable, like the changing seasons."

Cow deities are not demanding, let alone punishing, but rather indulgent and serving. This clearly distinguishes them from the ancient bull gods that represented boundless energy, manliness, and virility. Cow goddesses are unequivocally female but aren't overly sexed. Their femininity doesn't really extend beyond giving milk. They provide food, water, and warmth; they symbolize fertility, care, and life. In short, sacred cows and cow goddesses are almost clichéd mother figures or, as Mahatma Gandhi suggested, even über-mothers:

Our mother gives us milk for a couple of years and then expects us to serve her when we grow up. Mother cow expects from us nothing but grass and grain. Our mother often falls ill and expects service from us. Mother cow rarely falls ill . . . Our mother when she dies, means expenses of burial or cremation. Mother cow is as useful when dead as when she is alive.

But however motherly and profitable they may be, gods in animal form, including cow deities, have never had it easy in the Judeo-Christian world. The Israelites under Aaron—possibly remembering older Oriental deities—melted their gold jewelry. From it they fashioned a likeness of a calf to give thanks for their salvation from Egyptian bondage. Ever since, the proverbial "dance around the golden calf" has been used to describe profligate, money-grubbing behavior, and the worshipped animal became the epitome of an evil idol. "You shall not make for yourself an idol," says the first commandment, "of what is in heaven above or that on the earth beneath . . . You shall not worship them or serve them; for I, the LORD your God, am a jealous god." A notable deviation from this rule takes place during Carnival, when the foundations of the Christian world order are allowed to be shaken temporarily. On Mardi Gras, most notably in France and in Louisiana, a statue of a "fatted cow," the so-called *Boeuf Gras*, is dragged through the streets. In this case, the otherwise spurned "golden calf" is for once worshipped and celebrated in folkloristic Carnival celebrations.

The archetypical über-mother figure of Christianity (especially the Roman-Catholic variety), the Virgin Mary, also has striking similarities with the "heathen" cow goddesses of

Andrea di Lione, *Adoration of the Golden Calf*, oil on canvas
(17th century), Fine Arts Museums of San Francisco.

times past. In the Bible as well as in Catholic folk belief, the
Mother of God appears as a forceful and at the same time
quiet, humble, and devoted female figure. Mary, too, is female
in a motherly and caring rather than erotic and sexual way.
At the same time, the fact that she's female is an inalienable
aspect of her holiness. In the same way that the Egyptian
heavenly cow was regarded as the one who birthed the sun
god, Mary has been worshipped as the bearer of God since
the council of Ephesus in 431. In fact, a frequently occurring motif in Christian iconographic tradition is the image
of *Maria lactans*—that is, the Mother of God nursing Jesus. It
was presumably influenced by ancient Egyptian depictions
in which the goddess Isis, her head adorned with cow horns,
nurses her son Horus.

The parallels between cow, mother, and Mary are particularly obvious in a late-nineteenth-century painting by Italian symbolist Giovanni Segantini. Dominated by warm brown and ochre tones, the picture (one of the painter's most famous works) shows a woman in a stable, sitting on a stool. The only source of light is the lantern hanging in front of her. Her face, lit up by the light of the tallow candle, is turned toward the sleeping child in her arms. The woman is not explicitly identified as the Virgin Mary. But her humbly inclined head and the ambiance—a simple stable, just like the one in Bethlehem where Christ was born—are an unambiguous cross-reference to traditional depictions of the Mother of God. Like in the biblical Christmas story, the shed is full of animals. However, the one standing behind the woman at the manger is not an ox but a cow. Although the head of the cow almost vanishes in the semi-darkness, the lantern quite clearly illuminates her udder. To her left, on the straw, a calf is sleeping, just like the human child. The former also seems to just have been nursed, as the relatively small, apparently empty udder indicates.

On the whole, the painting exudes post-lactational serenity. Neither the woman nor the cow seems disturbed by the other's presence. They complement and reflect each other in a way. To the same degree that the cow is illuminated and elevated by the Mary-like woman, the woman is imbued with the character of Madonna by the bovine ambiance reminiscent of Bethlehem. The cow and the woman are equals in their role as child-bearing and nursing beings. As if concerned that the viewer might miss the parallels between madonna and vacca, Mother of God and mother cow, Segantini gave his painting the name Le due madri: "The two mothers."

Although we may interpret the Virgin Mary as a reincarnation and distant relative of pre-Christian cow goddesses,

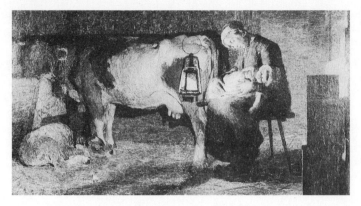

Giovanni Segantini, *Le due madri* (1889), oil on canvas,
Galleria d'Arte Moderna, Milano.

in the Western world domesticated cattle has undergone
a radical desecration since Auðumbla's times. "The cow,"
says Jeremy Rifkin, "once a god, was slowly transformed
into a commodity." She has descended from the pantheon
of natural gods into the lowlands of huge cowsheds and
slaughterhouses, no longer serving humans symbolically as a
nurturing mother goddess but literally at their disposal with
her milk, meat, and hide.

The progressive desecration of the cow reflects a fundamental change in the relationship between humans and
cattle or, more generally speaking, between humans and
nature. As Elias Canetti has shown, man tends to idolize animals that are more powerful than himself. "Those he cannot
subjugate, . . . he *venerates*." The fact that Neolithic hunters
and painters from today's Lascaux region covered the walls
of their caves with images of the wild, superhumanly strong
aurochs is testament to the reverence and deference they
showed toward that animal. The Sumerian, Egyptian, and
Germanic myths we saw above also describe a relationship

in which humans are dependent on the benevolence of ultimately unpredictable divine cattle.

If we invert the argument, Canetti's observation also suggests that what humans subjugate, they do not venerate. So
it's hardly surprising that in modern times domestic cattle—
systematically cultivated and physically as well as figuratively
put under the yoke by humans—have lost some of their divin-
ity in the course of progressive domestication. Ever since
Englishman Robert Bakewell and the Collins brothers laid
the foundations for modern cattle breeding in the eighteenth
century, the cow has increasingly become a functionally
differentiated human construct. Only because of human
breeding efforts do hundreds of cattle breeds exist today, their
various characteristics tailored to human needs (small horns,
high milk yield, lean meat). Today, high-performance cows of
the Holstein type give more milk in two weeks than average
early-nineteenth-century Prussian ones would produce in an
entire year. They are propagated mostly by artificial insemination or embryonic transfer. Particularly productive top-class
specimens—like Zita from Maryland, once a top-ranked dairy
cow—are occasionally even copied completely. Zita's clones,
Genesis Z and Cyagra Z, who were born to surrogate mothers in 2001, are her spitting image. Cows have long ceded
to be part of an unpredictable (let alone divinely created and
controlled) "natural" world and have become quintessential
products of human work and ingenuity. Human beings who
would revere our modern high-performance cows as deities
would be worshipping their own creations and therefore ultimately themselves.

But whom do cows look up to when they lament their
loss of meaning? To whom do they address their murmured,

mooing prayers when they lie in their pen in the shed at night, chewing cud? Whom do they beseech to make a miracle happen, when they see a full passenger train racing toward them? According to the ancient Greek philosopher Xenophanes of Colophon, the gods to whom cows pray have horns, udders, and a tail. After all, he writes, mortals also believe that their gods "wear their own clothes and have a voice and a body" just like themselves. Humans make their gods in their own image. "But if horses or oxen or lions had hands or could draw with their hands and accomplish such work as men, horses would draw the figures of the gods as similar to horses, and the oxen as similar to oxen, and they would make their bodies of the sort which each of them had." Humans have an anthropocentric view of the world—cows simply have a "bovicentric" one. Xenophanes's deliberations should be some consolation to cow deities. Even if humans in the Western world no longer pay them the respect they have been accustomed to since time immemorial, they can at least rely on their earthly fellow species, the more than one billion cloven-hoofed believers.

# EVIL COWS

TWO POINTED, curvy horns adorn the head. The hir-
sute body emits a pungent smell. A tail dangles from the
backside; the legs end in clunky cloven hooves. Many characteristics that apply to cows could well have been taken from
medieval depictions of the devil (although the goat-footed
god Pan might also have served as a model). The first official
description of the devil was published at the council of Toledo
in 447, and it was indeed based on the specific physique of
a cow. The latter was a central feature of the Mithras cult, a
serious competitor to Christianity in late-Roman times. By
declaring the holy animal of Mithraism a symbol of evil, "the
god of its adversary became the devil incarnate," says science
critic Jeremy Rifkin.

In the Middle Ages, the Horned One was sometimes also
referred to as "hellish cow." In a similar vein, the German
expression "black cow" was used to paraphrase impending
disaster or even witchcraft and dark magic. In the sixteenth century, Johann Baptist Fischart wrote about Pope Alexander VI:

*Monk-Calf of Freiberg*, by Lucas Cranach the Elder. This woodcut
appeared in an anti-Catholic pamphlet by Martin Luther and Philipp
Melanchthon. Luther claimed the birth of the deformed calf symbolized
the sin of the Catholic Church, while the Catholic Church countered
that it symbolized the sin of the Protestant Reformation (1523).

"After searching for strange agents for a long time, he finally
found none better than riding the black cow." To make quite
clear what he meant by this, the Calvinist poet and passionate
adversary of Catholicism made a note in the margin: "Pact of
the Pope with the devil."

Cows, bulls, and calves were not well regarded in Judeo-
Christian contexts, as they were sometimes revered as idols by
supporters of polytheistic religions and so were in direct com-
petition with the one, all-encompassing biblical God. What's
more, the *devil* = *cow* equation probably stems from the ana-
tomical similarities between the two creatures. If on top of

everything else the cow's coat was the same color as Satan's, according to Christian iconography, it may not have seemed too far-fetched to associate her with the powers of darkness. Apart from these physical features, the cow's character occasionally gave people pause. Cows were not always considered fundamentally good and patient creatures, let alone worshipped as motherly goddesses and saints. At times people had the sneaking suspicion that the cow's ostentatious calmness and friendliness might be nothing more than a clever act, a mask that could slip at any moment to reveal another as yet unknown and horrible face.

The writer (and former butcher) Beat Sterchi, for example, relates in *The Cow* that even in the twentieth century the idea of the "devil's cow" was still circulating among Swiss butchers. The cow devil was said to make cows that had already been stunned and stabbed inexplicably get up on their legs again. "The cow lifts her head. All wobbles and trembles: she pulls her weight onto her front feet. She is trying to get up. With nostrils dripping red, she trumpets through the slaughterhouse."

"Was her partial unpredictability the result of Manichean or Augustine devilry?" the author Thomas Kapielski asked after having spent a day mucking out in the cowshed, trying to understand the "singular behavior of cows." "Was it wily trickery with which they teased me, or pure coincidence and simple irregularity that at times they did what I expected them to do, other times and for the most exactly the opposite?" Are they in reality inwardly torn creatures, with only a thin veneer of civilization, or rather, domestication, preventing them from revealing their evil, devilish side to humans?

AMERICAN WRITER Ambrose Bierce apparently had no doubts whatsoever. His short story "Curried Cow" is about a cow that embodies absolute and inexplicable evil. The animal in question is called Phoebe. It supposedly belonged to the narrator's aunt Patience and lived in Michigan sometime in the nineteenth century:

> This creature was not a good cow, nor a profitable one. For instead of devoting a part of her leisure to the secretion of milk and the production of veal, she concentrated all her faculties on the study of kicking. She would kick all day and get up in the middle of the night to kick . . . It was pleasing to see her open a passage for herself through a populous barnyard. She would flash out, right and left, first with one hind leg and then with the other, and would sometimes, under favoring conditions, have a considerable number of domestic animals up in the air at once.

The cow might be named after a Greek moon goddess, but apart from that, Phoebe is anything but a saint. She's basically the antithesis of the good mother cow of antiquity or Hinduism, the adorable being that stands patiently in her shed, calves regularly, dutifully delivers her milk, and generally lets others do with her what they want. Strictly speaking, Phoebe is not a cow but a heifer—that is, a sexually mature female that hasn't had a calf yet. Phoebe is as unholy, as unfeminine, and in a way even as un-cow-like as a cow can possibly be.

The barnyard animals are not the only victims of her brutal kicks. The satanic heifer doesn't spare humans, either. The first task of every stableman who is taken into service by Aunt Patience is to currycomb the cow; and every single one of

them leaves with a limp in no time. The only one to succeed
in conquering evil and in taming the devilish cow is the good
Methodist preacher Huggins, whom Patience marries one day
after she has run out of stablemen. He puts up a man-sized
cast-iron pump in the middle of the yard and screws it onto
some huge wooden planks on the ground. Then he puts a hat
on the pump and covers it with a black frock coat so that, at
least to the blurry eyes of a cow, it looks like a priest.

The cow immediately sees her chance to destroy the puta-
tive Christian man whom she obviously views as a rival for her
mistress's affection. She approaches the pump-preacher with
great cunning. She pretends to not notice the gaunt creature
and strolls inconspicuously toward it. She sniffs the ground,
sticks her nose out to the cast-iron scarecrow, nods, blinks,
and smiles, as if she wants to be petted. And then she turns
around quick as lightning and deals the figure a "terrific blow"
with her hind legs.

> The effect was magical! Cows kick, not backward but
> sidewise. The impact which was intended to project the
> counterfeit theologian into the middle of the succeed-
> ing conference week reacted upon the animal herself and
> it and the pain together set her spinning like a top. Such
> was the velocity of her revolution that she looked like a
> dim circular cow, surrounded by a continuous ring like
> that of the planet Saturn—the white tuft at the extremity
> of her sweeping tail! Presently, as the sustaining centrifu-
> gal force lessened and failed . . . , she began to sway and
> wobble from side to side, and finally, toppling over on her
> side, rolled convulsively on her back and lay motionless
> with all her feet in the air . . . Then she fainted.

This Damascus Road experience seems to totally change Phoebe's character. Once she's become the unsuspecting victim of her own violence, she transforms from Saul into Paul. From then on, she is as "tractable and inoffensive . . . as a little child." She puts the leg, with which she used to kick so violently, into the preacher's lap. She is indeed so trusting that Patience's husband could take the leg "into his mouth," if only he wanted to. But then, one day, when Aunt Patience herself approaches the cow for the first time—up until then she has always sent the stablemen or her husband ahead—Phoebe suddenly shows her true, devilish face. With a violent kick, she smashes the old lady against the nearest wall, rendering her flat as a flounder. "You could not have done it so evenly with a trowel!" the narrator notes matter-of-factly.

"Curried Cow" is of course a satire. The image of a person spread in a thin layer on the face of a wall could have come from one of those comic strips that were popular in the U.S. in the late nineteenth century, when Bierce's story was published. Aunt Patience is the caricature of a withered old widow; her husband, the Reverend Berosus Huggins, a distorted picture of a Methodist lay preacher. And Phoebe, too, is vastly exaggerated. Of course there are stubborn, unpredictable cows that can deal rather painful blows. But they have no sinister strategy. They don't sneak up on their victims in a planned and deliberately inconspicuous way. They kick only when they feel frightened or threatened. As animals they are principally beyond moral categories such as good and evil.

Phoebe can be called an evil (or rather "not a good") cow in this story only because she's consistently anthropomorphized by the narrator and Aunt Patience, who is full of honest "love" for Phoebe and therefore avoids marriage for a long time. Phoebe finds being currycombed annoying. She is jealous of her mistress's new husband and is out to kill or at least harm him. The narrator tells us that she rubs her eyes in astonishment after she has lost the duel with the cast-iron dummy. Then she brokenheartedly retires to her shed.

In a way, Phoebe embodies all the negative character-istics that her owner lacks. She is, to use one of Carl Jung's expressions, Aunt Patience's "shadow," her evil antithesis, the incarnation of her suppressed personality. Like Dr. Jekyll and Mr. Hyde, Patience and Phoebe represent complemen-tary aspects of the same character. Aunt Patience is goodness and plainness incarnate; Phoebe is cunning and evil. Patience is, as her name implies, patient; Phoebe the epitome of sud-den, unmotivated violence. Patience would never mistreat her employees or fight with her husband; Phoebe does that on her behalf. With an alter ego like that, you can easily afford to be good all the time. However, to interpret the end of the story in another way, that kind of outsourcing of negative charac-teristics carries its own risks; your own "dark side" may well suddenly use its full power and smite you. The painstakingly constructed self-image of a good, peaceful person might all of a sudden get shattered on a nearby wall.

IN FACT, evil cows in literature and other types of discourse are normally projections. They are metaphors for events that actually play out in the human sphere—that is, an area where, in contrast to the animal kingdom, the categories "good" and "evil," "right" and "wrong" are quite legitimate. They often act as virtual scapegoats—or "scapecows"—for human errors. They personify grievances and catastrophes that would other-wise remain intangible and abstract.

For a few years now, for example, cattle have been considered "climate killers of the first order," as Bernhard Pötter put it in Die Zeit newspaper. The mastermind of this ecologically inspired demonization was, once again, Jeremy Rifkin. Adapting catastrophe-related imagery from the Old Testament, he had already referred to cows as "hoofed locusts" in the early 1990s: "More than a billion of these ancient ungulates roam the land today, trampling the soil, stripping everything bare and leaving a trail of destruction." According to Rifkin, modern cattle husbandry is "a new dimension of evil" in the world.

Cows do indeed contribute considerably to environmental pollution and destruction as well as to global climate change. Firstly, cattle husbandry is mainly responsible for the destruction of rainforests, especially in Central and South America. More and more trees fall victim to chainsaws and slash-and-burn to make space for cattle pastures or to create fields for feed, much of it for export. For each burger an estimated 65 square feet (6 square meters) of jungle have to give way.

Secondly, the principal cause for the worldwide spread of deserts, to which Rifkin alludes with his locust metaphor, is cattle husbandry. Free-grazing cattle eat approximately 880 pounds (400 kilos) of greens per month, trampling plants and soil in the process and thus contributing to the erosion and stripping of fertile topsoil. Africa, North America, and Australia are particularly affected by this. Furthermore, cows use vast amounts of water. In the United States, for example, half of the total water consumption is used to grow feed.

Thirdly, it's not just their hunger and thirst that makes cows responsible for the fact that water resources are running increasingly low. They also contaminate groundwater with cow pies. Worldwide, cow husbandry produces about one billion tons of organic waste per year; cattle consequently contribute approximately twice as much to the pollution of groundwater as the entirety of North American industries.

Fourthly and lastly, cows harm the global climate especially with the methane gas that forms in their stomachs during rumination. Methane is one of the most potent greenhouse gases. One methane molecule is over twenty times more effective at trapping the sun's heat than a molecule of carbon dioxide. Although comparatively rare in the atmosphere, methane contributes about one-fifth of the human- and cow-made greenhouse gas effect. As cows burp about every 40 seconds and emit up to 56 gallons (250 liters) of methane gas per day, they contribute to atmospheric heating on a massive scale; the greenhouse effect of cow burps amounts to about two billion tons a year. Likely nothing much will change until the portable "burp-trapping backpack" that scientists at the National Institute for Agricultural Technology in Buenos Aires have developed becomes commercially available.

Or (more realistically and yet fairly utopian) until more sustainable grazing practices are put into effect on a large scale. After all, grassland, if properly managed, has the potential to store vast amounts of carbon and thereby help combat global climate change. As Australian researcher Tony Lovell has shown, cattle grazing is not the problem per se. What's problematic is the overgrazing that has taken (and continues to take) place in many of the world's "brittle" regions—that is, pastures that receive little or no rainfall for long periods of time. Here, poor grazing practices often lead to an irreversible decline in the quality of top soil and ultimately to desertification, which in turn brings about the release of the carbon that has hitherto been stored in the soil. However, if

A cow sports a burp-trapping backpack, developed by scientists
at the National Institute for Agricultural Technology in Buenos Aires.

properly managed, Lovell argues, the roughly 12 billion acres
of arid pastureland that cover the earth could once again be
enabled to store large quantities of carbon and simultane-
ously be used for improved food production. "[T]he potential
is huge," writes British environmentalist Chris Goodall. "If
1 percent extra can be achieved across just half the world's
brittle lands, that would soak up the world's current emissions for over ten years."

Obviously, such a turn toward more sustainable land
management is not a decision that's for the cattle to make. In
2008, a large European energy company advertised its newly
built coal-fired power plant with the claim that "in contrast to
Veronica" the plant had "reduced its emissions considerably";
a photo of an innocent-looking calf was shown above it. The

little calf Veronica, the advertisement seems to imply, may be named after a Catholic saint and look at the viewer with sanctimonious eyes. But as it gets bigger, this calf, too, will grow devil's horns. At the end of the day, the lovable appearance of the young cow only masks a devious climate killer.

Of course it's not "Veronica's" fault that she burps methane. Nor are the close to 1.3 billion cattle that graze the earth to blame for the fact that in order to keep and feed them, forests are clear-cut, animal and plant species threatened, and vast quantities of water and energy spent. Morally responsible for this ecological aberration is the worldwide network of farmers, feed producers, slaughterhouses, leather manufacturers, beef eaters, milk drinkers, and other people involved in the global trade of cows—what Rifkin refers to as the "cattle complex." This kind of network is hard to untangle, and it's hard to blame anyone in particular. Because of this, and because most inhabitants of the Western world and emerging economies like China, India, or Brazil—be they producers or consumers—could probably be held responsible, the blame ultimately falls on the lowest common denominator for the complicated, unjust system: the evil cow; the hoofed locust; Veronica the climate killer. And because these creatures constitute metaphorical, if not mythical, entities, it's easy to push aside the question of guilt and responsibility and let the cattle complex prosper.

A SIMILAR kind of transference and personification of guilt took place during the BSE crisis that shook European beef eaters in the 1990s (and then quickly faded from public consciousness). BSE stands for bovine spongiform encephalopathy and describes a spongy degeneration in cattle brains.

The disease became known by the catchy colloquial name "mad cow disease."

The expression vividly and anthropomorphically hints at the symptoms of the illness: cows that have caught BSE behave as if they were "mad." They bellow constantly and without obvious reason; their bodies start jerking; in the terminal phase of the illness they suddenly collapse. The word "mad" here not only implies insanity but also "rage" and "evil." Cattle whose brains have been afflicted with BSE show unusually aggressive behavior, almost as if they were possessed by the devil. It was "really spooky," reported English vet David Bee, one of the first ones to observe the disease, "as if the cows had overly keen perception. They could recognize you from hundreds of yards away and would just go completely haywire." However, it wasn't the acute perception or the aggressiveness of the sick cattle that posed the greatest danger to humans but the consumption of their meat. BSE-contaminated meat is the most likely trigger of a deadly variant of Creutzfeldt-Jakob disease, to which dozens of people fell victim, especially in Great Britain.

British cows had been fed meat and bone meal processed from sheep carcasses and from other cows on a massive scale, and that's what is deemed to have caused the epidemic. Presumably some of the animals had been infected with scrapie, a disease similar to BSE that befalls sheep's brains. But tempers ran high not only because of the wantonly negligent handling of the contaminated meat and bone meal; it was the fact that animals had been fed to cows in the first place—that is, that cows, who are normally herbivores, had been fed meat. "Maybe the guilt starts much earlier," Barbara Supp wrote of the BSE scandal in *Der Spiegel* magazine, "maybe with the fact that cows were turned into cannibals." In April 1996 writer Julien Green noted in his journal: "Nowadays . . . cows are given feed which is made of animal matter, and then we talk about mad cows that have to be killed, because they are dangerous. That's how you turn herbivores into cannibals. Call that civilization?"

Interestingly enough the whole argument doesn't take place in the realm of natural sciences, such as epidemiology or agricultural sciences, but in the ethical sphere. From a scientific point of view, it would in principle be hard to argue against giving meat and bone meal to herbivores (as long as the meat hasn't been infected with germs, of course). Such practice wouldn't necessarily "diminish the well-being of cows," as animal ethicist Klaus Peter Rippe writes. The discontent and the pessimistic despair with civilization that's inherent in Julien Green's remarks must be attributed to our Western food taboos and moral ideas—and those are rooted in our culture, not in nature.

The first of these unwritten rules is that the meat of other carnivores is taboo. Those of us in the West who eat meat have an aversion to the meat of other meat eaters. Whether it's cows, pigs, sheep, or goats—all mammals that are normally part of our diet are vegetarians by nature. In contrast, dining on meat-eating animals such as dogs, cats, wolves, foxes, or rats is frowned upon.

The second, much stronger food taboo concerns consuming members of one's own species. Both Barbara Supp and Julien Green use the emotionally charged word "cannibal." Those who engage in cannibalism or turn other beings into cannibals—like those farmers who fed their cows the ground-up meat of other animals, including beef—find themselves on the margins of the Western world's moral rules.

Even worse, they shake the foundations of our culture. Nan Mellinger writes: "Cannibalism is used as a metaphor to emphasize the sanctity of the boundary between us and others, between humans and non-humans, between civilization and its resources."

By using the term "cannibalism" to refer to cows' consumption of meat and bone meal, Supp and Green transfer a human set of morals to cows, implying that they are somehow ethically responsible for the epidemic.

Just how deeply rooted the fear of carnivorous cows is, is apparent in the fact that the nightmarish motif has been haunting religion and literature for thousands of years. The first book of the Bible already gives an account of a herd of cannibalistic cows. Here, too, the animals appear on a purely symbolic level, as an allegory of the future of humankind. They graze and rage in one of the pharaoh's dreams at the time of the Israelites' Egyptian bondage. In his mythological trilogy *Joseph and His Brothers*, which is based on the biblical legend of Joseph, Thomas Mann renders this vision as follows: in his dream, the pharaoh is standing on the banks of the Nile, "in a lonely spot."

> Then he heard splashing not very far from the bank, and out of the flood seven shapes emerged—climbing on land were seven cows that must have been lying in the river the way water buffalo cows do, and they walked past, one after the other in single file, seven of them . . . Splendid cows—white, black, with a paler back, grey with a paler belly, and two dappled ones, splotched with markings—such beautiful, sleek and fat cows, with bulging udders and the heavily lashed eyes of Hathor, and tall, curved, lyre-shaped horns; and they began to graze contentedly

The pharaoh has a dream about cannibalistic cows
in this illustration from the Morgan Bible (c. 1240).

among the reed grass. The king had never seen such magnificent cattle.

But the king's pleasure in watching the splendid cows doesn't
last long. As soon as the animals emerge from the water,
seven more follow—and they are a lot more unsightly than
the previous ones:

Pharaoh shuddered at these cattle, they were the ugliest, leanest, gauntest cows he had ever seen in his life—their bones stuck out under their wrinkled hide, their udders were empty sacks with teats like cord . . . the miserable creatures seemed scarcely able to stay on their feet; but their behavior was shamelessly impudent, viciously hostile, quite out of keeping with their frailty . . . As Pharaoh watches the wretched herd attack the sleek one: the hideous cows climb onto the beautiful ones, the way cows do when they play bull; then the wretched animals devour the splendid ones, wolf them down, simply wipe the meadow clean of them.

It's hardly surprising that the sovereign seeks an explanation for this disturbing dream, more so when it's reinforced by a second, similar vision (in which full and empty ears of cereal replace the cows). Unfortunately, none of the local soothsayers and sages manages to interpret the nightmare scenario to his satisfaction. One conjectures that the seven beautiful cows represent the pharaoh's daughters, who must all die during the sovereign's lifetime. Another speculates they stand for his male descendants, who will be dethroned by seven "princes of wretched lands." A third one claims they are seven queens whom the pharaoh will take into his "house of women" and who unfortunately would not live long either.

In his despair the pharaoh eventually sends for the boy Joseph, a slave from Judah who is said to have unusual interpretative skills. And indeed, Joseph has an explanation: the seven beautiful and the seven ugly cows represent seven years, respectively—the beautiful cows stand for the rich, fertile years, the ugly ones for the following epoch of deprivation and hunger. So the pharaoh would be well advised to make provisions for the future. During each of the fat years he should have a fifth of the harvest collected and stored in large granaries so that, as the Bible says, "let the food become as a reserve for the land for the seven years of famine which will occur in the land of Egypt, so that the land will not perish during the famine."

In contrast to Genesis, where the description of the pharaoh's dream is a lot shorter, Thomas Mann emphasizes the status of the seven beautiful cows by giving them not just bulging udders but also the lashed "eyes of Hathor"—eyes that mark them as divine animals. The fact that they emerge from the river Nile, whose floods were indispensible for Egyptian agriculture, identifies the cows as givers of blessings and providers of food.

But then the inconceivable happens. The divine animals disappear, down the throats of the other cows, of all things. Significantly, these "ugly" cows, like the cow Phoebe in Ambrose Bierce's story, lack any motherly or feminine features. "Their udders," Mann writes, "look like empty sacks with teats like cord" and their "behavior" is not caring but murderous. Like fallen angels they attack their "sisters" and eat them in a way that has the characteristics of a cannibalistic coitus. In a culture that is shaped by cattle husbandry and worship, there can hardly be a more impressive image for a threatening ecological and economical catastrophe, for a world that is out of joint.

THE FACT that the image of the cannibalistic cow still sparks outrage about the feeding of meat and bone meal to cattle and the fact that most people don't want to acknowledge how ecologically damaging the mass husbandry of cattle is, both point to the idea that we actually don't really believe that cows could have bad character traits. We don't accord them the slyness that would be needed to produce truly criminal energy. Nor can we rid ourselves of the millennia-old idea of a selflessly caring, gentle, motherly nurturer. As paradoxical as this may sound, cows are simply too good to be truly evil. If cows behave badly, it's either because they are symbolic "scapecows" for human wrongdoings or because they are "possessed" in the religious or scientific sense: by the cow devil or the pathogens of bovine spongiform encephalopathy. Or because they are symbols for another grievance, such as a threatening famine.

They might have a physical resemblance to the devil of Christian popular belief, but cows don't stand a chance against other animal incarnations of the old tempter. At times they even seem involuntarily laughable in their attempts to do something evil. In the *Far Side* cartoon "Sunday morning in the Garden," Gary Larson uses a Holstein to directly contrast cows and evil. Adam and Eve, still naked and oblivious, walk in the Garden of Eden. Sitting on a tree in the shape of a snake, Satan offers them an apple. One treetop further sits a devil-horned cow, shouting, "Peaches! I got niiiiiiice fresh peaches!" Adam and Eve's decision is well known. Despite all the cow's other talents, the sly, evil temptress isn't a role she can really pull off.

# APOCALYPSE COW

NYONE WHO'S ever read through the Apocalypse of Saint John or watched a Hollywood movie about the impending end of the world knows that during the last days of humankind all kinds of animals and animal-like creatures will emerge: monsters, devils, dragons with ten horns, four-headed panthers with bird wings—but cows? Prim as cows normally are in the pasture, you hardly expect them to play a special role in the horrors and carnage of the end time. And yet, they keep on showing up in works about the apocalypse.

"Apocalypse Cow" was a headline in the German weekly *Die Zeit* in April 2001. It was the height of foot-and-mouth disease, which in England alone cost more than 6 million cattle their lives. Under the headline was a photo of a pyre on which the cows' cadavers were being burned. *Die Zeit's* unusually cabaret-style headline was obviously an allusion to the title of Francis Ford Coppola's famous 1979 antiwar movie *Apocalypse Now*. Whereas Coppola's masterpiece about the Vietnam War deals with American GIs, North Vietnamese jungle fighters, and civilians, the article in Die Zeit is "merely" about sick cows. But the subliminal message in both cases is very similar. Under the fragile varnish of human civilization the potential for violence and unimaginable horror still lurks. A heart of darkness beats in the bodies of seemingly civilized people. Cleansing and sacrificial rituals reminiscent of the Middle Ages continue to exist even in modern and postmodern times. As the theologian Georg Pfleiderer remarked with regard to the pyre photograph and its headline in Die Zeit:

> The combination of images of the inferno with sacrificial semantics . . . dramatically illuminates the apocalypse: the sacrificial semantics is heightened into an image of Armageddon . . . The return of the sacrificial rites that the modern era had seemingly eliminated is a premonitory announcement . . . of the end of this era.

The death of millions of cattle and their incineration on a massive scale thus seem to foreshadow the end of civilization. What prosaically speaking is nothing more than a cruel but temporary agricultural policy measure is heightened into an end-of-days massacre.

The expression "Armageddon" that Pfleiderer uses comes from the last book of the Bible, the Apocalypse of Saint John. It refers to the location of the battle "of the Great Day of God Almighty," one of the last confrontations between the powers of God and those of darkness. In the course of this battle very heavy hailstones fall from the sky, a massive tremor shakes the earth, islands disappear beneath the surface of the sea, and mountains collapse. Shortly after that, the city of Babylon—the epitome of earthly sinfulness—is razed to the ground. The Antichrist has to admit defeat; the dead arise from their graves and the Last Judgment takes place. This is the end of the world as we know it. "Then I saw a new heaven and a new earth," it says in the Apocalypse of Saint John, "because the first heaven and the first earth had disappeared, and the sea was gone."

Despite the catastrophic cow epidemics of the late second and early third millennium CE, the world has not yet come to an end. And yet, it's fascinating that we assign so much importance to cows that we interpret their mass slaughter as a warning sign, a bad omen for our own survival. But if we consider that to the ancient Egyptians the cow was a precondition for life on earth and that in Germanic mythology the divine cow Auðumbla marked the beginning of time and human civilization, it's not that surprising that the cow's demise is so closely associated with our own and that she should be present at the end of time. Her return at the end of the world is consistent with philosopher Karl Löwith's idea that world history is just a big detour that at the end of time leads back to its beginning.

Cows have always been harbingers of the apocalypse. Not when they graze peacefully on the pastures but when they show unnatural or even perverse behavior—and most of all, when they leave their ancestral place on God's green earth and abruptly take flight, be it with the help of a crane that lifts them onto the pyre or by other means.

"THIS IS what things have come to in this world. The cows sit on the telegraph poles and play chess." These are the first lines of Dadaist poet Richard Huelsenbeck's poem "The End of the World," published in 1919 in the magazine Der

Cows culled in the foot-and-mouth disease outbreak in
Great Britain are prepared for incineration.

*Dada.* The doomsday mood of World War I was the historical background for this work—and for the emergence of the
Dada movement in general, which had begun three years earlier in the Cabaret Voltaire in Zurich. Huelsenbeck describes
the mood as a "feeling of terror," "an existential despair" to
which the Dadaists reacted with "creative irrationalism."

The image of the cows sitting on telegraph poles playing
chess expresses this irrationalism in a concise yet desperately
funny way. A touch of irony is added by the indignant bourgeois exclamation "This is what things have come to in this
world," as if chess-playing cows were just more proof of general moral decline. At the same time the image lends itself
to political interpretation. After all, chess is nothing but
a war game in the course of which kings must be protected,
knights positioned, and pawns sacrificed. The fact that this

power game is played by cows of all species, cows that sit on long-distance communication lines with their broad behinds, speaks volumes about the catastrophic state of the world.

At the same time, castling cows at airy heights can look back to a long ancestral line of strange metaphors that predate Dadaism by centuries. For example, the German expression "the cow walks on stilts," an allegory for a world turned upside down, dates back to the late seventeenth century. "The cow will dance on a rope, the ox will understand Latin" had a similar meaning. In the English nursery rhyme "Hey Diddle Diddle," which dates back to the eighteenth century, a cow is even said to jump "over the moon"—one of several images of inexplicable but endearing oddness. All these expressions share the idea of cows suddenly taking to giddy heights where they perform high-wire (or high-jumping or stilt-walking) acts that proclaim an out-of-whack or even upside-down world order. If a very heavy animal like the cow, which is not exactly known for its artistic subtleness, acts counter to all known patterns of behavior and maybe even defies the basic laws of physics, we may well say that strange things are happening on earth.

ALTHOUGH MOST of these expressions are no longer in common usage, the absurd and even disturbing image of cows balancing at great heights or flying through the air still lingers in today's cultural memory. It's interesting that the image recurs in connection with collapses or catastrophes of civilization. At the beginning of *Apocalypse Now*, for example, a brutal assault of American soldiers on a Vietnamese village is followed by a scene in which a cow is taken away in a helicopter. She seems to be part of the American war booty; stealing

The cow jumps over the moon in "Hey Diddle Diddle"—
a sign of a world turned upside down?

her is clearly an offense against the rules of martial law. While an army chaplain celebrates mass in the foreground, the cow—hanging helplessly from a rope under the helicopter—disappears into the air in the background. Her mooing blends with the voices of the chaplain and a handful of his flock as they recite the Lord's Prayer. In this instance, Christian ritual, in the form of a desperate evocation of moral norms, is foiled by a violation of rules and the aerial animal sacrifice.

A similar haul takes place in Steven Spielberg's movie *Jurassic Park*, set on an island-turned–supposedly safe dinosaur park, where a cow is lifted into a cage full of velociraptors with the help of a giant cable winch. What happens afterwards remains invisible for the spectators (those in the movie as well as those in the movie theater). But the cow's death roar leaves no doubt that an uncontrollable and bestial elemental force reigns at the lower end of the rope, within the shadows of the dense, tropical canopy. And lo and behold: shortly afterwards, nature, genetically mutated and abused by humankind, strikes back. Together with a few specimens of *Tyrannosaurus rex* and other maladjusted pets, the predatory dinosaurs break out of their high-security cages and give the humans who get in their way the same treatment they gave the cow.

And finally, in a key scene of the disaster movie *Twister*, a cow is yanked up into the air by an approaching tornado, presumably an allusion to the children's classic *The Wizard of Oz*. *Twister* is actually about a couple of meteorologists and their daring research into super-tornados. But many spectators view this sequence as the climax of the entire movie and the cow as its real star. The apocalyptic force of the tornado manifests itself in a grotesque way that is both convincing and aesthetically captivating. In its clutches even a cow—and an especially large-framed and heavy Holstein at that—can effortlessly be wrenched from the powers of gravity.

All these scenes have one thing in common: the catastrophic destiny of the cows foreshadows that of humans. Captain Willard, the protagonist of *Apocalypse Now*, will very shortly also have the rug pulled from under his feet. Most of those watching the feeding of the velociraptors will not survive their visit to Jurassic Park. The super-tornado not only sucks up the cow but also the small town of Wakita, Oklahoma, which is now home to a *Twister* museum, replete with flying-cow memorabilia. You could say that when cows go to heaven, humans will usually follow without delay. Another feature these films share is that the events they describe are "apocalyptic" only in a larger, colloquial sense. Although they portray catastrophes that may seem like end-of-days events to the people and cows involved, history and the world at large continue to run their course.

British author Douglas Adams took a much more radical approach to this idea. In his comical science-fiction epic *The Hitchhiker's Guide to the Galaxy*, a four-volume "trilogy in five parts," he actually describes the end of the world, the absolute end of time. And there again, of course, at the end of time, a cow is waiting.

ACCORDING TO Douglas Adams the end of the world happens every evening. It's the main attraction and unique selling point of the restaurant Milliways, also known as "The Restaurant at the End of the Universe," which gave the second volume of the *Hitchhiker's* trilogy its title. The restaurant is built on the fragmented remains of a destroyed planet "which is enclosed in a vast time bubble and projected forward in time to the precise moment of the End of the Universe." Again and again enormous "Time Turbines" slowly rock it over the edge of time and, lucky for the restaurant patrons, quickly back again. The establishment is thus constantly perched at the end of the world. Protected by the cupola's energy shield, visitors can enjoy their dinner while watching the demise of the universe. However, the most astonishing thing about this restaurant—or at least the one that shakes the trilogy's protagonist to the core—is not the breathtaking spectacle of "livid, swollen stars" that will go out any minute but the sight of the main course.

The main course of the Last Day is a cow: "a large fat meaty quadruped of the bovine type with large watery eyes, small horns and what might almost have been an ingratiating smile on its lips." We can assume that the animal is the result of billions of years of efforts to create a low-maintenance beef cattle breed. The actual breeding success, though, lies hidden behind the watery eyes and winning smile. The cow hasn't just been bred to be eaten—she *wants* to be eaten, and she can clearly express this wish:

> "Good evening," it lowed and sat back heavily on its haunches, "I am the main Dish of the Day. May I interest you in parts of my body?" . . . "Or the rump is very good," murmured the animal. "I've been exercising it and eating plenty of grain, so there's a lot of good meat there." It gave a mellow grunt, gurgled again and started to chew the cud. It swallowed the cud again.

The polite Brit Arthur Dent is appalled when he hears the dinner invitation from the victim's mouth. The argument that it's better to eat an animal that *wants* to be eaten than, say, a head of lettuce that does *not* want to be eaten doesn't sway him. This is where Zaphod Beeblebrox, the galaxy's president, takes command:

> "Four rare steaks, please, and hurry. We haven't eaten in five hundred and seventy-six thousand million years." The animal staggered to its feet. It gave a mellow gurgle. "A very wise choice, sir, if I may say so. Very good!" it said, "I'll just nip out and shoot myself." He turned away and gave a friendly wink to Arthur. "Don't worry, sir," he said, "I'll be very humane."

And indeed, shortly afterwards a waiter appears bearing four juicy, steaming steaks.

The cow in this example is the caricature of a docile, meek sacrificial animal. The creation of a breed that wants to be eaten is of course a deliberately outrageous fantasy and so is clearly and excessively satirized. But Adams addresses a moral problem that has accompanied humans from the very beginning and will probably stay with them until the end of time: the dilemma that in order to stay alive, we have to constantly incur guilt. We can't eat without killing an animal or at least wrenching a poor head of lettuce from the vegetable patch. The optimistic vision of the end of the world that Adams projects in this story finally removes the sting of this ethical problem. The Restaurant at the End of the Universe is a truly "heavenly" place where humans and animals live together in harmony and the former can eat the latter without scruples.

But in order to do so they first have to swap roles. The cow's last words are, "I'll be very humane." In the context of the book, this is obviously supposed to mean, "I will kill myself in a humane way." At the same time, a second meaning is clearly audible: I will be very human. By committing an act that is normally the prerogative of humans—that is, by taking my own life—I become human. In this version of the end of the world, the cow adopts surprisingly human traits. The humans, in contrast, who simply accept her death and eat her without thinking, look like animals (or, in the case of Zaphod Beeblebrox, like a two-headed extraterrestrial). As soon as the cow moves into higher spheres, the world order is once again turned upside down.

THE COW is dead, long live the cow. Her flesh is made into juicy steaks and eaten. Her skin is made into leather, her horns are fashioned into combs and buttons, her eyes end up on the dissecting table in high-school biology courses. What remains? In light of all the cows that rove about at airy heights at the end of the world, be it on telegraph poles, tightropes, or in the ruins of the planet Frogstar World B, we have to ask ourselves what actually happens to them after their death, other than being processed by humans. Do cows belong to the "righteous" in the sense of Saint John's apocalypse? Is their name recorded in the "Book of Life"? In other words: do cows, since they seem to prefer the heavenly spheres during the apocalypse anyway, go to heaven?

Among theologians the question of whether animals go to heaven was a point of controversy for a long time. The church father Aurelius Augustine roundly excluded animals from the Christian resurrection community, because he believed that they have no soul. Saint Thomas Aquinas, too, believed that neither plants nor animals have a place in heaven. Only Martin Luther speculated during one of his table talks that there might be a spot in paradise reserved for animals. "Heaven does not just mean air and land, or what is above us, but also everything that is part of it, all cattle, small animals, and so on." According to the reformer, honest domestic animals like cows would actually make up a majority in heaven. This is because God has mitigated Adam and Eve's punishment for their misdemeanor and the ensuing Fall by stocking the worldly realm with "more animals that are useful and serve us than animals that harm us"—that is, "more oxen than lions; more cows than bears."

From the point of view of well-meaning humans—and surely that of cows, too—the ascension of cows to heaven must be highly desirable. As writer Eckhard Henscheid puts it: "The mere sight of grazing and resting and ruminating cows awakens and stokes in us the constricting and irrepressible longing for a future encounter with them in the other world." A nice thought in principle, but are such aesthetic pleasures enough to give cows the right of access to heaven, a decision that, at least in the case of humans, is made based on moral criteria?

Henscheid's argument that cows should "on account of their especially difficult labor go to heaven" seems more convincing. In the Christian world great suffering has always been known as a tried and tested means to reach the kingdom of heaven. And anyone who has ever heard the bloodcurdling roar of a cow giving birth can't doubt that cows are especially worthy of ascending to heaven. Against this backdrop the seemingly radical adage of the naturalistic poet Conrad Alberti makes sense. He postulated that the "birth-throes of a cow" are equivalent to the "death of a great hero." The suffering she endures while giving birth to a little calf is hardly easier and sometimes maybe even much more prolonged than that of a dying hero—and the humility with which cows take their suffering is no less admirable. In a sense, cows atone for the fall of our ancestors by doing so. As we know, labor is the punishment that God inflicted for the progressive curiosity of the primordial mother Eve. Men were punished with having to work in the fields. And the cows and oxen that are used as draft animals traditionally also carry the burden of this curse on their broad backs.

In the case of the "daily special" in Douglas Adams's *Restaurant at the End of the Universe*, the cow seems almost Christlike. By voluntarily and ungrudgingly sacrificing her body and blood for hungry humans, she embodies the *imitatio christi*, the Imitation of Christ, like early Christian and medieval martyrs. "May I interest you in parts of my body?" is a polite version of the call to Holy Communion as issued by Christ in the Gospel of Matthew: "Take, eat; this is my body."

THE POEM "Das Kalb" (The calf) by Swabian writer Justinus Kerner, written one and a half centuries before Adams's trilogy, points in a similar direction:

> Dear calf, you were born in a shed in the dark,
> You hardly have time to be gay.
> The butcher, he grasps you, so cold in his heart,
> From your mother he tears you away.
>
> So bright, so pious shine your large eyes,
> The moment they see the green lea.
> The dogs' vicious barking soon darkens your skies
> How frightened you are, woe is thee.
>
> And soon they will bind your frail legs with a rope,
> No matter how fearful your cry.
> Once thrown on the shambles, you will have no
>     more hope.
> They will cut through your throat and you'll die.
>
> But with your last breath I can quite clearly see
> Your eyes speaking, shiny and awed:
> "I too have a soul that's alive within me.
> I too will be judged by a god."

The preordained life journey of the young cow is obviously a kind of Via Dolorosa. And there are indeed hints that point toward a certain similarity in nature between the calf and the crucified one. Like the infant Jesus, it's born in a "dark stable," between ox and donkey; and the intimacy between mother and child is highlighted by the brutal act of the calf's being wrenched from her.

Of course, that doesn't make the calf the son of God (who preferably appears as a lamb when taking the metaphoric guise of an animal). But it does have the features of a righteous human being (in the sense of the Saint John apocalypse) who is chosen for suffering. Its eyes are "pious." It's bound by its persecutors (a choice of words again reminiscent of the suffering of Christ as described in Luther's Bible translation). Finally, at the moment of death, its eyes emit a brightness that testifies to the fact that its soul has just left it; that, just like humans, it will participate in the divine Last Judgment after its death or at the end of the world. It's safe to say that the verdict for the young cow will point toward heaven. Apart from the fact that cows are peaceable and fundamentally good animals anyway, the calf, after all, had no chance to sin, because it went directly from the manger to the slaughterhouse without ever becoming aware of the seductive possibilities that life offers. If such an animal doesn't go to heaven, then nobody deserves it.

We can thus justifiably assume that the happy hunting pasture of the afterlife will resonate not only with the flutter and singing of angels but also with the odd blissful moo. In his vision of a future messianic kingdom, the prophet Isaiah already saw cows as the epitome of natural and peaceful coexistence, as a model for all those carnivorous predators that bring death and damnation to their fellow beings in this world: "Calves and lions will eat together and be cared for by little children. Cows and bears will graze the same pasture, their young will lie down together, and lions will eat straw like cattle." That's a prospect that should allow us to face our own death and, should it come to that, the end of the world, with equanimity.

# NOTES

The numbers on the left refer to page numbers.

IN THE BEGINNING WAS THE COW

1 New American Standard Bible (© 1995), Genesis 1:22 and 1:26.

2 Michael Brackmann, *Das andere Kuhbuch: Vierzig Rasseporträts und mehr.* Hannover: Landbuch, 2002: p. 7.

2 Jeremy Rifkin, *Beyond Beef: The Rise and Fall of the Cattle Culture.* New York: Plume, 1993: p. 17.

6 Eckhard Fuhr, "Die Leiden der jungen Muhkuh." *Die Welt,* August 1, 2007.

6 Johann Gottfried Ebel, *Schilderung der Gebirgsvölker der Schweitz.* Leipzig: Pet. Phil. Wolfische Buchhandlung, 1798: p. 79.

8 Robert Musil, *The Man without Qualities,* Vol. 1 and 2. Vintage, 1996.

8 Frédéric Boyer, *Vaches.* Paris: P.O.L., 2008.

8 Elisabeth von Tadden and Ulrich Schnabel, "Die Kühe haben das Wort. Gene, Tiermehl und andere Mitbürger: Ein Gespräch mit dem Wissenschaftsforscher Bruno Latour." *Die Zeit,* November 30, 2000: pp. 67–68.

9 Julius Caesar, *The Gallic Wars.* St. Petersburg, FL: Red & Black Publishers, 2008: p. 167.

11 Johann Wolfgang von Goethe, "On Myron's Cow." *American Journal of Philology,* Vol. 131, No. 4, Winter 2010: pp. 725–729.

A KINGDOM FOR A COW

12 Pat Paulsen, "Two Cows." *Pat Paulsen for President* (Audio CD). Laugh.com/ Fontana, 2003.

13 Jeremy Rifkin, *Beyond Beef: The Rise and Fall of the Cattle Culture*. New York: Plume, 1993.

13 Jacob Grimm, *The Complete Grimm's Fairy Tales*. Hollywood, FL: Simon & Brown, 2011: pp. 14–15.

17 Otto Schrader, quoted in Wilhelm Gerloff, *Die Entstehung des Geldes und die Anfänge des Geldwesens*. Frankfurt am Main: Vittorio Klostermann, 1940: p. 104.

17 Sir Walter Scott, *The Waverley Novels*. London: A&C Black, 1866: p. 63.

18 Karl Marx, *Capital: A Critique of Political Economy—Vol. 1, Part 1: The Process of Capitalist Production*. New York: Cosimo Inc., 2007: pp. 94, 173.

18 Cornelius Tacitus, *Agricola and the Germania*. New York: Penguin Classics, 2010: pp. 104–105.

20 Ovid, *Metamorphoses: A New Translation by Charles Martin*. New York: W.W. Norton & Company, 2005: pp. 40, 80.

20 Friedrich Hebbel, "Die Kuh." *Werke*, Vol. 3. Munich: Hanser, 1965: pp. 489–493.

24 Kurt Weill and Robert Vambery, *Der Kuhhandel: Auszüge*. Königsdorf: Capriccio, 1992.

26 Hermann Essig, *Die Glückskuh*. Leipzig: Kurt Wolff, 1918.

FLESH AND BLOOD

29 François Rabelais, *Gargantua and Pantagruel*. Project Gutenberg Ebook 1200, Book 11, chapter 2, IV.

31 Jeremy Rifkin, *Beyond Beef: The Rise and Fall of the Cattle Culture*. New York: Plume, 1993: pp. 155–156.

32 Jacques Derrida, *Points...Interviews, 1974–1994*. Palo Alto, CA: Stanford University Press, 1995: p. 281.

32 Den Fujita, quoted in Jeremy Rifkin, *Beyond Beef: The Rise and Fall of the Cattle Culture*. New York: Plume, 1993: p. 271.

33 Roland Barthes, *Mythologies*. New York: Farrar, Straus & Giroux, 1972: p. 62.

33 Bertolt Brecht, *Saint Joan of the Stockyards*. Bloomington: Indiana University Press, 1970: p. 64.

34 Beat Sterchi, *The Cow*. New York: Pantheon Books, 1988: p. 109.

34 Nan Mellinger, *Fleisch: Ursprung und Wandel einer Lust*. Frankfurt am Main and New York: Campus, 2003.

34 Petronius Arbiter, *The Satyricon of Petronius*. Charleston, SC: Forgotten Books, 1971: pp. 71–72.

35 Bertolt Brecht, *Threepenny Opera*. New York: Grove Press, 1964: p. 27.

36 Gary Larson, *The Complete Far Side*, Vol. 1. Riverside, NJ: Andrews McMeel, 2003: p. 406.

38 Jochen F. Fey, "Kochkunst auf der documenta XII: Gedanken zum 'Kochen' und zur 'Kunst.' " *journal culinaire: Kultur und Wissenschaft des Essens* 5 (November 2007): pp. 49–52.

38 François Rabelais, *Gargantua and Pantagruel*. Project Gutenberg Ebook 1200, Book II, chapter 2, IV.

MILK

39 Vilém Flusser, "Kühe." *Vogelflüge: Essays zu Natur und Kultur.* Munich and Vienna: Hanser, 2000: p. 44–48.

40 "Council Regulation (EEC) No. 1898/87 of 2 July 1987 on the protection of designations used in marketing of milk and milk products." eur-lex. europa.eu/LexUriServ/LexUriServ.do?uri=CELEX:31987R1898:EN:HTML.

41 Michael Brackmann, *Kuhkunstführer*. Münster: Landwirtschaftsverlag, 2006.

42 Thomas Hardy, *Tess of the d'Urbervilles*. Reprint Services Cooperation, 2007: pp. 141–142.

43 Rolf Husmann, in Andreas Kronenberg and Rolf Husmann. "Nuer (Ostafrika, Oberer Nil): Tägliche Arbeiten im Viehlager." *Encyclopaedia Cinematographica*. Göttingen: Institut für den Wissenschaftlichen Film, 1976: Film E 706/1964.

44 Mahatma Gandhi, *The Story of My Experiments with Truth*. Boston: Beacon Press, 1993: p. 454.

44 Thomas Dineley, in A.T. Lucas. *Cattle in Ancient Ireland*. Kilkenny: Boethius, 1989: p. 56.

45 Barthold Heinrich Brockes, "Die Heerde Kühe." *Irdisches Vergnügen in Gott, bestehend in Physikalisch- und Moralischen Gedichten*, Vol. 2. Hamburg: Herold et al., 1735–48 [1970]: pp. 201–202.

49 William Shakespeare, *Macbeth*, Act 1, Scene 5, 15–18.

49 New American Standard Bible (© 1995), Exodus 33:3.

50 Sigmund Freud, *Civilization and Its Discontents*. New York: W.W. Norton, 1961. ia600301.us.archive.org/34/items/CivilizationAndItsDiscontents/ freud_civilization_and_its_discontents.pdf.

51 Heinz Strunk, *Fleisch ist mein Gemüse: Eine Landjugend mit Musik*. Reinbek bei Hamburg: Rowohlt, 2004.

51 Dieter Schnack and Rainer Neutzling, quoted in Lothar Schon, *Entwicklung des Beziehungsdreiecks Vater-Mutter-Kind*. Stuttgart: Kohlhammer, 1995: p. 123.

51 From *Poems of Paul Celan*, translated by Michael Hamburger. Translation copyright © 1972, 1980, 1988, 2002 by Michael Hamburger. Reprinted by permission of Persea Books, Inc., New York.

52 Rose Ausländer, "Ins Leben." *Gesammelte Werke*, Vol. 1. Frankfurt am Main: Fischer, 1985: p. 66.

52 Robert Johnson, "Milk Cow's Calf Blues." *The Complete Recordings*, CBS, 1990.

53 Norbert Kaser, "eine kuh." *es bockt mein herz: Überlebenstexte*. Leipzig: Reclam, 1993: pp. 55–56.

HIDE AND HAIR

56 Barthold Heinrich Brockes, "Die Heerde Kühe." *Irdisches Vergnügen in Gott, bestehend in Physikalisch—und Moralischen Gedichten*, Vol. 2. Hamburg: Herold et al., 1735–48 [1970]: pp. 201–202.

58 Arnold Stadler, *Mein Hund, meine Sau, mein Leben*. Frankfurt am Main: Suhrkamp, 1996.

UDDER AND VULVA

72 *Time Magazine*, quoted in Sean Griffin, *Tinker Bells and Evil Queens*. New York: New York University Press, 2000.

72 Magnus Hirschfeld, ed., *Geschlecht und Verbrechen*. Leipzig and Vienna: Schneider & Co., 1930.

73 New American Standard Bible (© 1995), Leviticus 20:15, 20:16.

75 Peter Stierli, quoted in Stephanie Riedi, Roland Grüter, and Tom Haller, "Stalldrang." FACTS, September 16, 1998: pp. 104–109.

77 Alan Lomax, "I'm Bound to Follow the Longhorn Cows." *The Folk Songs of North America*. Garden City, NY: Doubleday & Co., 1960: p. 368.

81 Ernst Jandl, "seichende kuh." *Poetische Werke*. Munich: Luchterhand Literaturverlag, 1997: p. 132.

82 Ovid, *The Art of Love*. New York: Liveright Publishing Corporation, 1943: p. 24.

83 Botho Strauß, *The Park*. Sheffield: Sheffield Academic Press, 1988: pp. 65–66.

83 Michael Brackmann, *Kuhkunstführer*. Münster: Landwirtschaftsverlag, 2006.

84 Ovid, *The Art of Love*. Liveright Publishing Corporation, 1943: p. 26.

84  Keith O'Brien, quoted in "Cardinal O'Brien Condemns 'Monstrous' Embryo Research." 4RFV, March 21, 2008, www.4rfv.co.uk/nationalnews. asp?id=73347.

84  Peter Michalski, "Forscher züchten ersten Kuh-Menschen." Bild, April 2, 2008, www.bild.de/news/vermischtes/beruehmte-deutsche-forscher/von-forschern-gezuechtet-4167794.bild.html.

84  Lyle Armstrong, quoted in "U.K. Approves Human-Animal Hybrids." Cosmos, September 6, 2007, www.cosmosmagazine.com/news/1564/uk-approves-human-animal-hybrids.

THE EYE

88  Johann Baptist Fischart and Jakob Böhme, quoted in Jacob and Wilhelm Grimm, "Kuh," Deutsches Wörterbuch, Vol. 11. Leipzig: S. Hirzel, 1854–1960: pp. 2546–2551.

88  Richard Marius, Martin Luther: The Christian between God and Death. Cambridge, MA: Harvard University Press, 1999: p. 75.

88  Johann Baptist Fischart and Jakob Böhme, quoted in Jacob and Wilhelm Grimm, "Kuh," Deutsches Wörterbuch, Vol. 11. Leipzig: S. Hirzel, 1854–1960: pp. 2546–2551.

88  Otto Dornblüth, Klinisches Wörterbuch. Berlin and Leipzig: deGruyter, 1927.

88  Sigmund Freud, Dora: An Analysis of a Case of Hysteria. New York: Touchstone, 1997: p. 71.

89  Meredith Etherington-Smith, The Persistence of Memory: A Biography of Dalí. Cambridge, MA: Da Capo Press, 1995: p. 102.

90  William Hazlitt, The Plain Speaker: The Key Essays. Hoboken, NJ: Wiley-Blackwell, 1999: p. 133.

90  Martin Buber, I and Thou. London: Continuum International Publishing Group, 2004: p. 73.

90  Hellmut von Cube, "Die Kühe." Tierskizzenbüchlein. Berlin: S. Fischer, 1935: pp. 20–23.

91  Beat Sterchi, The Cow. Pantheon Books, 1988: pp. 350–351.

92  Martin Mosebach, Das Beben. Munich: Hanser, 2005.

95  Jakob von Uexküll, A Foray into the Worlds of Animals and Humans with a Theory of Meaning. Minneapolis: University of Minnesota Press, 2010: p. 69.

95  Temple Grandin, Animals in Translation: Using the Mysteries of Autism to Decode Animal Behavior. Fort Washington, PA: Harvest Books, 2006: p. 8.

97  John Ruskin, The Elements of Drawing. London: Smith, Elder & Co., 1857.

HAPPINESS THROUGH RUMINATION

100  Heinrich Böll, *Irish Journal*. Evanston, IL: Northwestern University Press, 1998: p. 42.

101  Thomas Bewick, *A General History of Quadrupeds*, 3rd edition. Newcastle: Newcastle upon Tyne, 1792: p. 23.

101  D.H. Lawrence, "Love Was Once a Little Boy." In Susan J. Armstrong and Richard G. Botzler, eds., *The Animal Ethics Reader*. London and New York: Routledge, 2003: pp. 104–105.

102  Joachim Ringelnatz, "Kühe." *Die Gedichte*. Frankfurt am Main: Zweitausendeins, 2005: p. 274.

102  Hellmut von Cube, "Die Kühe." *Tierskizzenbüchlein*. Berlin: S. Fischer, 1935: pp. 20–23.

103  British Organic Milk Suppliers Cooperative, www.love-om.com/om-tea-break-meditation.ashx. Accessed October 28, 2008.

105  Barthold Heinrich Brockes, "Die Heerde Kühe." *Irdisches Vergnügen in Gott, bestehend in Physikalisch—und Moralischen Gedichten*, Vol. 2. Hamburg: Herold et al., 1735–48 [1970]: pp. 201–202.

105  Robert Musil, "Grigia." In Eithre Wilkins and Ernst Kaiser, *Five Women by Robert Musil*. Boston: David R. Godine Publisher, 1999: p. 27.

107  Augustine, *Confessions*. New York: Penguin Classics, 1961: pp. 220–221.

108  Gary Larson, *The Complete Far Side*, Vol. 1. Riverside, NJ: Andrews McMeel, 2003: p. 160.

108  Friedrich Nietzsche, *Untimely Meditations*. Cambridge: Cambridge University Press, 1997: p. 60.

110  Friedrich Nietzsche, *Thus Spoke Zarathustra*. Plain Label Books, 1967: pp. 411–412, 414–416, 307.

HERDING COWS

113  Theocritus, Tyrtaeus, James Davies, Richard Polwhele, and Matthew James Chapman, *The Idylls of Theocritus, Bion and Moschus and the War-Songs of Tyrtaeus*. London: H.G. Bohn, 1870: pp. 104–105.

114  Alexander Pope, "Winter. The Fourth Pastoral, or Daphne." John Butt, ed. *The Poems of Alexander Pope*. Abingdon: Routledge, 1963: pp. 135–139.

115  Mönch von Salzburg, "Das kchühorn." In Martina Backes, ed. *Tagelieder des deutschen Mittelalters*. Stuttgart: Reclam, 1992: pp. 204–207.

118  Johann Gottfried Ebel, *Schilderung der Gebirgsvölker der Schweitz*. Leipzig: Pet. Phil. Wolfische Buchhandlung, 1798: p. 79.

120  Achim von Arnim and Clemens Brentano, "Emmenthaler Kühreihen." *Des Knaben Wunderhorn: Alte Deutsche Lieder*, Vol 3. Stuttgart: Reclam, 2006: pp. 130–131.

122  John Gay, *The Shepherd's Week*. London: Jacob Tonson, 1721: p. 18.
122  Heinrich Heine, *The Poems of Heine*. London: George Bell & Sons, 1887: p. 554.
124  Wilhelm Busch, *Balduin Bählamm, der verhinderte Dichter*. Munich: Verlag Fr. Bassermann, 1911, pp. 32–33.

THE MOO

128  Michel Houellebecq, *Whatever*. London: Serpent's Tail, 1998: p. 8.
128  Virgil, *The Works of Virgil*, Vol. 2. New York: T&J Swords, 1811: p. 238.
129  Giorgio Agamben, *Infancy and History: The Destruction of Experience*. London: Verso, 1993: p. 61.
130  Melanie Feist, *Untersuchungen zum Schmerzausdrucksverhalten bei Kühen nach Klauenoperationen*, deposit.d-nb.de/cgi-bin/dokserv?idn=97250172x&dok_var=d1&dok_fpr=md5&filename=d-nb.d5.txt.
131  Ovid, *Metamorphoses*. Cambridge, MA: Hackett Publishing, 2010: pp. 24, 303.
133  Aeschylus, *Prometheus Bound*. Mundelein, IL: Bolchazy-Carducci Publishers, 1990: p. 51.
134  Ovid, *Metamorphoses*. Cambridge, MA: Hackett Publishing, 2010: pp. 28–29.
134  New American Standard Bible (© 1995), Matthew 12:34.
134  Amos Tutuola, *The Palm-Wine Drinkard and My Life in the Bush of Ghosts*. New York: Grove Press, 1993: pp. 44, 47, 49.

BEHIND THE FENCE

139  Beat Sterchi, *The Cow*. New York: Pantheon Books, 1988: p. 5.
140  Bertolt Brecht, "Cow at Cud." *Ars Interpres—Journal of Poetry, Translation and Art*, No. 3, 2004: p. 28.
141  Beat Sterchi, *The Cow*. New York: Pantheon Books, 1988: p. 54.
142  Michael Brackmann, *Das andere Kuhbuch: Vierzig Rasseporträts und mehr*. Hannover: Landbuch, 2002.
143  Temple Grandin, *Animals in Translation: Using the Mysteries of Autism to Decode Animal Behavior*. Fort Washington, PA: Harvest Books, 2006: p. 247.
143  Elias Canetti, *Crowds and Power*. New York: Farrar, Straus & Giroux, 1984: p. 53.
144  James Harrington, *The Commonwealth of Oceana*. Glasgow and New York: Routledge, 1887 : p. 116.
144  Bertolt Brecht, *Saint Joan of the Stockyards*. Bloomington: Indiana University Press, 1970: p. 29.
144  Alfred Döblin, *Berlin Alexanderplatz*. London: Continuum International Publishing Group, 2004: p. 103.

145 Johann Gottfried Ebel, *Schilderung der Gebirgsvölker der Schweitz*. Leipzig: Pet. Phil. Wolfische Buchhandlung, 1798: p. 79.

149 Thomas Kapielski, *Danach war schon: Gottesbeweise I–VIII*. Berlin: Merve, 1999.

149 Zwi Bacharach, in interview. "Witnesses and Testimony, " *Yad Vashem*, www1.yadvashem.org/yv/en/education/ceremonies/witness_testimony.asp.

149 Thomas Kapielski, *Danach war schon: Gottesbeweise I–VIII*. Berlin: Merve, 1999.

151 Vilém Flusser, "Kühe." *Vogelflüge: Essays zu Natur und Kultur*. Munich and Vienna: Hanser, 2000: p. 44–48.

153 Walter Kaufmann, ed., *The Portable Nietzsche*. New York: Penguin Books, 1977: p. 383.

SACRED COWS

156 Mahatma Gandhi, in Steven J. Rosen, *Holy Cow: The Hare Krishna Contribution to Vegetarianism and Animal Rights*. Herndon, VA: Lantern Books, 2004: p. 37.

157 Mahatma Gandhi, *Speeches and Writing of M.K. Gandhi*. Charleston, SC: Nabu Press, 2010: p. 830.

157 Paul Bowles, *Their Heads Are Green and Their Hands Are Blue*. New York: Random House, 1963: pp. 57–58.

158 Marvin Harris, et al., "The Cultural Ecology of India's Sacred Cattle." *Current Anthropology* 7 (1966): pp. 51–60.

159 Clemens Six, "'Hinduise all Politics & Militarize Hindudom!!' Fundamentalismen im Hinduismus." In Clemens Six, Martin Riesebrodt and Siegfried Haas, eds., *Religiöser Fundamentalismus: Vom Kolonialismus zur Globalisierung*. Innsbruck: Studien, 2005: pp. 247–268.

160 Tierno Monénembo, *Peuls*. Paris: Éditions du Seuil, 2004.

161 Snorri Sturluson, *The Prose Edda: Norse Mythology*. New York: Penguin Classics, 2006: p. 15.

161 Jeremy Rifkin, *Beyond Beef: The Rise and Fall of the Cattle Culture*. New York: Plume, 1993: p. 25.

162 K.S. Bharathi, *The Social Philosophy of Mahatma Gandhi*. Concept Publishing Company, 1991: p. 75.

162 New American Standard Bible (© 1995), Exodus 20:4, 20:5.

165 Jeremy Rifkin, *Beyond Beef: The Rise and Fall of the Cattle Culture*. New York: Plume, 1993: p. 32.

165  Elias Canetti, *Crowds and Power*. New York: Farrar, Straus & Giroux, 1984: p. 372.

167  Xenophanes of Colophon, *Fragments*. Toronto: University of Toronto Press, 2001: pp. 83, 89.

EVIL COWS

168  Jeremy Rifkin, *Beyond Beef: The Rise and Fall of the Cattle Culture*. New York: Plume, 1993: p. 23.

169  Martin Luther, quoted in Jacob and Wilhelm Grimm, "Kuh," *Deutsches Wörterbuch*, Vol. 11. Leipzig: S. Hirzel, 1854–1960: pp. 2546–2551.

170  Beat Sterchi, *The Cow*. New York: Pantheon Books, 1988: pp. 121, 92.

170  Thomas Kapielski, *Danach war schon: Gottesbeweise I–VIII*. Berlin: Merve, 1999.

171  Ambrose Bierce, *The Complete Stories of Ambrose Bierce*. Lawrence, KS: Digireads.com Publishing, 2008: pp. 273, 279, 276.

175  Bernhard Pötter, "Klimakiller ersten Ranges." *Die Zeit*, January 18, 2007: p. 21.

175  Jeremy Rifkin, *Beyond Beef: The Rise and Fall of the Cattle Culture*. New York: Plume, 1993: pp. 186, 284.

177  Chris Goodall. *Ten Technologies to Save the Planet*. Vancouver, BC: Greystone, 2010: p. 263.

179  David Bee, quoted in Barbara Supp, "Auch Minister haben Angst." *Der Spiegel*, October 5, 1998: pp. 126–132.

179  Barbara Supp, "Rinderwahn." *Der Spiegel*, October 5, 1998. www.spiegel.de/spiegel/print/d-8002705.html.

180  Julian Green, quoted in Iris Radisch, "Der Kuhhandel der Werte: Warum Julien Green den BSE Skandal nicht versteht." *Die Zeit*, November 30, 2000: p. 27.

180  Klaus-Peter Rippe, "Schadet es Kühen, Tiermehl zu fressen?" In Martin Liechti, ed., *Die Würde des Tieres*. Erlangen: Harald Fischer, 2002: pp. 233–242.

181  Nan Mellinger, *Fleisch: Ursprung und Wandel einer Lust*. Frankfurt am Main and New York: Campus, 2003.

181  Thomas Mann, *Joseph and His Brothers*. New York: Everyman's Library, 2005: pp. 1131–1132.

184  New American Standard Bible (© 1995), Genesis 41:36.

184  Thomas Mann, *Joseph and His Brothers*. New York: Everyman's Library, 2005: p. 1139.

185 Gary Larson, *The Complete Far Side*, Vol. 1. Riverside, NJ: Andrews McMeel, 2003: p. 549.

APOCALYPSE COW

187 Georg Pfleiderer, "Theologische Überlegungen zur Wahrnehmung von Tieren in der Moderne." In Martin Liechti, ed. *Die Würde des Tieres.* Erlangen: Harald Fischer, 2002: pp. 47–60.

187 New American Standard Bible (© 1995), Book of Revelation 16:14, 21:1.

188 Robert Motherwell, *The Dada Painters and Poets: An Anthology.* Cambridge, MA: Harvard University Press, 1989: p. 226.

188 Richard Huelsenbeck, *Memoirs of a Dada Drummer.* Berkeley: University of California Press, 1991: p. 145.

193 Douglas Adams, *The Restaurant at the End of the Universe.* New York: Picador, 1980: pp. 80, 83, 93, 94, 95–96.

196 Martin Luther, *Sämtliche Schriften*, Vol. 22: *Colloquia oder Tischreden.* Groß Oesingen: Heinrich Harms, 1987.

196 Eckhard Henscheid, *Welche Tiere und warum das Himmelreich erlangen können: Neue theologische Studien.* Stuttgart: Reclam, 1995.

197 Conrad Alberti, quoted in Harvey W. Hewett-Thayer, *The Modern German Novel: A Series of Studies and Appreciations.* Manchester, NH: Ayer Publishing, 1977: p. 81.

197 New American Standard Bible (© 1995), Matthew 26:26.

198 Justinus Kerner, "Das Kalb," *Werke*, Vol. 1, Berlin: Bong & Co, 1914: p. 179.

199 New American Standard Bible (© 1995), Isaiah 11:6.

# BIBLIOGRAPHY

Abrams, Meyer H. "Apocalypse: Theme and Variations." In C.A. Patrides and Joseph Wittreich, eds. *The Apocalypse in English Renaissance Thought and Literature*. Ithaca: Cornell University Press, 1984: pp. 342–368.

Adams, Douglas. *The Restaurant at the End of the Universe*. New York: Picador, 1980.

Aeschylus. *Prometheus Bound*. Translated by Paul Roche. Mundelein, IL: Bolchazy-Carducci Publishers, 1990.

Agamben, Giorgio. *Infancy and History: The Destruction of Experience*. Translated by Liz Heron. London: Verso, 1993.

Augustine. *Confessions*. Translated by R.S. Pine-Coffin. New York: Penguin Classics, 1961.

Ausländer, Rose. "Ins Leben." *Gesammelte Werke*, Vol. 1. Frankfurt am Main: Fischer, 1985.

Bacharach, Zwi. "Witnesses and Testimony." *Yad Vashem*, www1. yadvashem.org/yv/en/education/ceremonies/witness_testimony.asp.

Barthes, Roland. *Mythologies*. Translated by Richard Howard. New York: Farrar, Straus & Giroux, 1972.

Bewick, Thomas. *A General History of Quadrupeds*, 3rd edition. Newcastle: Newcastle upon Tyne, 1792.

Bharathi, K.S. *The Social Philosophy of Mahatma Gandhi*. New Delhi: Concept Publishing Company, 1991.

Bierce, Ambrose. *The Complete Stories of Ambrose Bierce*. Lawrence, KS: Digireads.com Publishing, 2008.

Böll, Heinrich. *Irish Journal*. Translated by Leila Vennewitz. Evanston, IL: Northwestern University Press, 1998.

Borchmeyer, Dieter. "Der Naturalismus und seine Ausläufer." In Viktor Žmegač, ed. *Geschichte der deutschen Literatur vom 18. Jahrhundert bis zur Gegenwart*, Vol. 2. Königstein: Athenäum, 1980: pp. 153–178.

Bowles, Paul. *Their Heads Are Green and Their Hands Are Blue*. New York: Random House, 1963.

Boyer, Frédéric. *Vaches*. Paris: P.O.L., 2008.

Brackmann, Michael. *Das andere Kuhbuch: Vierzig Rasseporträts und mehr*. Hannover: Landbuch, 2002.

———. *Kuhkunstführer*. Münster: Landwirtschaftsverlag, 2006.

Brecht, Bertolt. "Cow at Cud." Translated by Augustus Young. *Ars Interpres—Journal of Poetry, Translation and Art*, No. 3, 2004: p. 28.

———. *Saint Joan of the Stockyards*. Translated by Frank Jones. Bloomington: Indiana University Press, 1970.

———. *Threepenny Opera*. Translated by Ralph Manheim and John Willett. New York: Grove Press, 1964.

Brockes, Barthold Heinrich. "Die Heerde Kühe." *Irdisches Vergnügen in Gott, bestehend in Physikalisch—und Moralischen Gedichten*, Vol. 2. Hamburg: Herold et al., 1735–48 [1970]: pp. 201–202.

Brocks, Christine. *Die Kuh—die Milch*. Dresden: Deutsches Hygiene-Museum, 1997.

Buber, Martin. *I and Thou*. Translated by Walter Kaufmann. London: Continuum International Publishing Group, 2004: p. 73.

Busch, Wilhelm. *Balduin Bählamm, der verhinderte Dichter*. Munich: Verlag Fr. Bassermann, 1911, pp. 32–33.

Butt, John, ed. *The Poems of Alexander Pope*. Abingdon; Routledge, 1963.

Caesar, Julius. *The Gallic Wars*. Translated by W.A. McDevitt and W.S. Bohn. St. Petersburg, FL: Red & Black Publishers, 2008.

Canetti, Elias. *Crowds and Power*. Translated by Carol Steward. New York: Farrar, Straus & Giroux, 1984.

"Cardinal O'Brien Condemns 'Monstrous' Embryo Research." 4RFV, March 21, 2008, www.4rfv.co.uk/nationalnews.asp?id=73347.

Catlette, Bill, and Richard Hadden. *Contented Cows Give Better Milk*. Saltillo Press, 1998.

———. *Contented Cows Moove Faster*. R. Brent & Co., 2007.

Celan, Paul. *Poems of Paul Celan: A Bilingual German/English Edition*. Translated by Michael Hamburger. New York: Persea Books, 2002.

Charisius, Hanno. "Embryo aus Mensch und Kuh: Briten schaffen Mischwesen für die Stammzellforschung." *Süddeutsche Zeitung*, April 3, 2008: p. 18.

Dalí, Salvador. *Das geheime Leben des Salvador Dalí*. Munich: Schirmer und Mosel, 1984.

Datta, Venita. "A Bohemian Festival: La Fête de la Vache Enragée." *Journal of Contemporary History* 28 (1993): pp. 195–213.

Derrida, Jacques. *Points... Interviews, 1974–1994*. Translated by Peggy Kamuf et al. Palo Alto, CA: Stanford University Press, 1995.

Dineley, Thomas. "Observations in a Voyage through the Kingdom of Ireland, 1680." *Journal of Kilkenny and South-East of Ireland Archaeological Society*, new ser., 1 (1856–1857).

Döblin, Alfred. *Berlin Alexanderplatz*. Translated by Eugène Jolas. London: Continuum International Publishing Group, 2004.

Dornblüth, Otto. *Klinisches Wörterbuch*. Berlin and Leipzig: deGruyter, 1927.

Duve, Karen, and Thies Völker. *Lexikon berühmter Tiere*. Frankfurt am Main: Eichborn, 1997.

Ebel, Johann Gottfried. *Schilderung der Gebirgsvölker der Schweitz*. Leipzig: Pet. Phil. Wolfische Buchhandlung, 1798.

Eberle, Ute. "Die Kuh ist tot, es lebe die Kuh!" *Die Zeit*, February 21, 2002: pp. 31–32.

Eichinger Ferro-Luzzi, Gabriella. *The Self-Milking Cow and the Bleeding Lingam: Criss-Cross of Motifs in Indian Temple Legends*. Wiesbaden: Otto Harrassowitz, 1987, pp. 107–108.

Eisenstein, Sergei. *Strike*. Soviet Union, 1925.

Essig, Hermann. *Die Glückskuh*. Leipzig: Kurt Wolff, 1918.

Etherington-Smith, Meredith. *The Persistence of Memory: A Biography of Dalí*. Cambridge, MA: Da Capo Press, 1995.

Feist, Melanie. *Untersuchungen zum Schmerzausdrucksverhalten bei Kühen nach Klauenoperationen*, deposit.d-nb.decgi-bin/dokserv?idn= 97250172x&dok_var=d1&dokfpr=md5&filename=d-nb.d5.txt.

Felius, Marleen. *Cattle Breeds: An Encyclopedia*. North Pomgret, VT: Trafalgar Square Books, 2007.

Fey, Jochen F. "Kochkunst auf der documenta XII: Gedanken zum 'Kochen' und zur 'Kunst.'" *journal culinaire: Kultur und Wissenschaft des Essens* 5 (November 2007): pp. 49–52.

Flusser, Vilém. "Kühe." *Vogelflüge: Essays zu Natur und Kultur*. Munich and Vienna: Hanser, 2000: p. 44–48.

Freud, Sigmund. *Civilization and Its Discontents.* Translated by James Strachey. New York: W.W. Norton, 1961.

———. *Dora: An Analysis of a Case of Hysteria.* New York: Touchstone, 1997.

Fuhr, Eckhard. "Die Leiden der jungen Muhkuh." *Die Welt,* August 1, 2007.

Gandhi, Mahatma. *Speeches and Writing of M.K. Gandhi.* Charleston, SC: Nabu Press, 2010.

Gandhi, Mahatma. *The Story of My Experiments with Truth.* Boston: Beacon Press, 1993.

Gay, John. *The Shepherd's Week.* London: Jacob Tonson, 1721: p. 18.

Gerloff, Wilhelm. *Die Entstehung des Geldes und die Anfänge des Geldwesens.* Frankfurt am Main: Vittorio Klostermann, 1940.

Goethe, Johann Wolfgang von. "On Myron's Cow." *American Journal of Philology,* Vol. 131, No. 4 (Whole Number 524), Winter 2010: pp. 725–729.

Goodall, Chris. *Ten Technologies to Save the Planet.* Vancouver, BC: Greystone, 2010.

Grandin, Temple. *Animals in Translation: Using the Mysteries of Autism to Decode Animal Behavior.* Fort Washington, PA: Harvest Books, 2006.

Griffin, Sean. *Tinker Bells and Evil Queens.* New York: New York University Press, 2000.

Grimm, Jacob. *The Complete Grimm's Fairy Tales.* Hollywood, FL: Simon & Brown, 2011.

Grimm, Jacob and Wilhelm. "Die Kuh." *Deutsches Wörterbuch,* Vol. 11. Leipzig: S. Hirzel, 1854–1960: pp. 2546–2551.

Guggenbühl, Dietegen. *Mit Tieren und Teufeln: Sodomiten und Hexen unter Basler Jurisdiktion in Stadt und Land 1399 bis 1799.* Basel: Verlag des Kantons Basel-Landschaft, 2002.

Hardy, Thomas. *Tess of the d'Urbervilles.* Reprint Services Cooperation, 2007.

Harrington, James. *The Commonwealth of Oceana.* Glasgow and New York: Routledge, 1887.

Harris, Marvin, et al. "The Cultural Ecology of India's Sacred Cattle." *Current Anthropology* 7 (1966): pp. 51–60.

Harris, Marvin. *Wohlgeschmack und Widerwillen: Die Rätsel der Nahrungstabus.* Stuttgart: Klett-Cotta, 1991.

Hazlitt, William. *The Plain Speaker: The Key Essays.* Hoboken, NJ: Wiley-Blackwell, 1999.

Hebbel, Friedrich. *Die Kuh. Werke,* Vol. 3. Munich: Hanser, 1965: pp. 489–493.

Heine, Heinrich. *The Poems of Heine*. Translated by Edgar Alfred Bowring. London: George Bell & Sons, 1887.

Henscheid, Eckhard. "Wiedersehenstränen." *Sentimentale Tiergeschichten*. Stuttgart: Reclam, 1997: pp. 271–272.

———. *Welche Tiere und warum das Himmelreich erlangen können: Neue theologische Studien*. Stuttgart: Reclam, 1995.

Hewett-Thayer, Harvey W. *The Modern German Novel: A Series of Studies and Appreciations*. Manchester, NH: Ayer Publishing, 1977.

Hirschfeld, Magnus, ed. *Geschlecht und Verbrechen*. Leipzig and Vienna: Schneider & Co., 1930.

Hornung, Erik. *Der Ägyptische Mythos von der Himmelskuh: Eine Ätiologie des Unvollkommenen*. Freiburg, CH: Universitätsverlag, and Göttingen: Vandenhoeck & Ruprecht, 1982.

Houellebecq, Michel. *Whatever*. Translated by Paul Hammond. London: Serpent's Tail, 1998.

Huelsenbeck, Richard. *Memoirs of a Dada Drummer*. Translated by Joachim Neugroschel. Berkeley: University of California Press, 1991.

Jandl, Ernst. "seichende kuh." *Poetische Werke*. Munich: Luchterhand Literaturverlag, 1997: p. 132.

Jha, D.N. *The Myth of the Holy Cow*. London and New York: Verso, 2002.

Johnson, Robert. "Milk Cow's Calf Blues." *The Complete Recordings*, CBS, 1990.

Junghänel, Frank. "Das hat gerade noch gefehlt." *Berliner Zeitung*, May 20, 2006: M06.

Kapielski, Thomas. *Danach war schon: Gottesbeweise I–VIII*. Berlin: Merve, 1999.

Kaser, Norbert. "eine kuh." *es bockt mein herz: Überlebenstexte*. Leipzig: Reclam, 1993: pp. 55–56.

Kaufmann, Walter, ed. *The Portable Nietzsche*. Translated by Walter Kaufmann. New York: Penguin Books, 1977.

Kerner, Justinus. "Das Kalb." *Werke*, Vol. 1, Berlin: Bong & Co, 1914: p. 179.

Kinsey, Alfred Charles. *The Sexual Behavior in the Human Female*. Bloomington: Indiana University Press, 1998.

———. *The Sexual Behavior in the Human Male*. Bloomington: Indiana University Press, 1998.

Kronenberg, Andreas, and Rolf Husmann. "Nuer (Ostafrika, Oberer Nil): Tägliche Arbeiten im Viehlager." *Encyclopaedia Cinematographica*. Göttingen: Institut für den Wissenschaftlichen Film, 1976: Film E 706/1964.

Larson, Gary. *The Complete Far Side*, vol. 1. Riverside, NJ: Andrews McMeel, 2003.

Lawrence, D.H. "Love Was Once a Little Boy." In Susan J. Armstrong and Richard G. Botzler, eds. *The Animal Ethics Reader*. London and New York: Routledge, 2003: pp. 104–105.

Lomax, Alan. "I'm Bound to Follow the Longhorn Cows." *The Folk Songs of North America*. Garden City, NY: Doubleday & Co., 1960: p. 368.

Lucas, A.T. *Cattle in Ancient Ireland*, Kilkenny: Boethius, 1989, p. 56.

Luther, Martin. *Sämtliche Schriften*, Vol. 22: *Colloquia oder Tischreden*. Groß Oesingen: Heinrich Harms, 1987.

Mann, Thomas. *Joseph and His Brothers*. Translated by John E. Woods. New York: Everyman's Library, 2005.

Marius, Richard. *Martin Luther: The Christian between God and Death*. Cambridge, MA: Harvard University Press, 1999.

Marx, Karl. *Capital: A Critique of Political Economy—Vol. 1, Part 1: The Process of Capitalist Production*. New York: Cosimo Inc., 2007.

———. *Marx on Religion*. John C. Raines, ed. Philadelphia: Temple University Press, 2002.

Mellinger, Nan. *Fleisch: Ursprung und Wandel einer Lust*. Frankfurt am Main and New York: Campus, 2003.

Menninghaus, Winfried. *Disgust: Theory and History of a Strong Sensation*. Albany: State University of New York Press, 2003: p. 208.

Michalski, Peter. "Forscher züchten ersten Kuh-Menschen," Bild, April 2, 2008, www.bild.de/news/vermischtes/beruehmte-deutsche-forscher/von-forschern-gezuechtet-4167794.bild.html.

Mönch von Salzburg. "Das Kchühorn." In Martina Backes, ed. *Tagelieder des deutschen Mittelalters*. Stuttgart: Reclam, 1992: pp. 204–207.

Monénembo, Tierno. *Peuls*. Paris: Éditions du Seuil, 2004.

Mosebach, Martin. *Das Beben*. Munich: Hanser, 2005.

Motherwell, Robert. *The Dada Painters and Poets: An Anthology*. Cambridge, MA: Harvard University Press, 1989.

Müns, Heike, ed. *Ein paar hundert ausgewählte alte und neue Strophen von Herrn Pasturn sien Kauh*. Rostock: VEB Hinstorf, 1984.

Musil, Robert. *The Man without Qualities*, Vol. 1 and 2. Translated by Sophie Wilkins and Burton Pike. New York: Vintage, 1996.

———. "Grigia." In Eithre Wilkins and Ernst Kaiser, *Five Women by Robert Musil*. Translated by Eithre Wilkins and Ernst Kaiser. Boston: David R. Godine Publisher, 1999.

New American Standard Bible (© 1995).

Nietzsche, Friedrich. *Untimely Meditations.* Translated by R.J. Hollingdale. Cambridge: Cambridge University Press, 1997.

———. *Thus Spoke Zarathustra.* Translated by Thomas Common. Charleston, SC: Plain Label Books, 1967.

Ovid. *Metamorphoses.* Translated by Stanley Lombardo. Cambridge, MA: Hackett Publishing, 2010.

———. *Metamorphoses: A New Translation by Charles Martin.* New York: W.W. Norton & Company, 2005.

———. *The Art of Love.* Translated by Christopher Marlowe. New York: Liveright Publishing Corporation, 1943.

Paulsen, Pat. "Two Cows." *Pat Paulsen for President* (Audio CD). Laugh.com/ Fontana, 2003.

Petronius Arbiter. *The Satyricon of Petronius.* Translated by Alfred A. Allison. Charleston, SC: Forgotten Books, 1971.

Pfleiderer, Georg. "Theologische Überlegungen zur Wahrnehmung von Tieren in der Moderne." Martin Liechti, ed. *Die Würde des Tieres.* Erlangen: Harald Fischer, 2002: pp. 47–60.

Plinius Secundus d. Ä. "[Myron]." *Naturkunde.* Munich and Zurich: Artemis, 1989: p. 49.

Pötter, Bernhard. "Klimakiller ersten Ranges." *Die Zeit,* January 18, 2007: p. 21.

Rabelais, François. *Gargantua and Pantagruel.* Translated by Sir Thomas Urquhart of Cromarty and Peter Antony Motteux. Project Gutenberg Ebook 1200, Book II, chapter 2, IV.

Radisch, Iris. "Der Kuhhandel der Werte: Warum Julien Green den BSE Skandal nicht versteht." *Die Zeit,* November 30, 2000: p. 67.

Riedi, Stephanie, Roland Grüter and Tom Haller. "Stalldrang." FACTS, September 16, 1998: pp. 104–109.

Rifkin, Jeremy. *Beyond Beef: The Rise and Fall of the Cattle Culture.* New York: Plume, 1993.

———. "Klimawandel und Hunger: Der Wahnsinn mit den Rindern." *Süddeutsche Zeitung,* August 5, 2008: p. 2.

Ringelnatz, Joachim. "Kühe." *Die Gedichte.* Frankfurt am Main: Zweitausendeins, 2005: p. 274.

Rippe, Klaus-Peter. "Schadet es Kühen, Tiermehl zu fressen?" In Martin Liechti, ed. *Die Würde des Tieres.* Erlangen: Harald Fischer, 2002: pp. 233–242.

Rosen, Steven J. *Holy Cow: the Hare Krishna Contribution to Vegetarianism and Animal Rights.* Herndon, VA: Lantern Books, 2004.

Rousseau, Jean-Jacques. *A Dictionary of Music.* Translated by William Waring. Florence, KY: Gale ECCO Print Editions, 2010.

Ruskin, John. *The Elements of Drawing.* London: Smith, Elder & Co., 1857.

Schon, Lothar. *Entwicklung des Beziehungsdreiecks Vater-Mutter-Kind.* Stuttgart: Kohlhammer, 1995.

Scott, Sir Walter. *The Waverley Novels.* London: A&C Black, 1866.

Seiler, Herbert. "Blaue Milch—gibt es die wirklich? Blaue Milch durch eine Biovariante von Pseudomonas fluorescens." *Deutsche Molkereizeitung* 12 (2006): pp. 25–27.

Shakespeare, William. *Macbeth.*

Six, Clemens. "'Hinduise all Politics & Militarize Hindudom!!' Fundamentalismen im Hinduismus." In Clemens Six, Martin Riesebrodt, and Siegfried Haas, eds. *Religiöser Fundamentalismus: Vom Kolonialismus zur Globalisierung.* Innsbruck: Studien, 2005: pp. 247–268.

Stadler, Arnold. *Mein Hund, meine Sau, mein Leben.* Frankfurt am Main: Suhrkamp, 1996.

Sterchi, Beat. *The Cow.* Translated by Michael Hoffmann. New York: Pantheon Books, 1988.

Strauß, Botho. *The Park.* Translated by Tinch Minter and Anthony Vivis. Sheffield: Sheffield Academic Press, 1988.

Strunk, Heinz. *Fleisch ist mein Gemüse: Eine Landjugend mit Musik.* Reinbek bei Hamburg: Rowohlt, 2004.

Sturluson, Snorri. *The Prose Edda: Norse Mythology.* Translated by Jesse L. Bycock. New York: Penguin Classics, 2006.

Supp, Barbara. "Auch Minister haben Angst." *Der Spiegel,* October 5, 1998: pp. 126–132.

———. "Rinderwahn." *Der Spiegel,* October 5, 1998. www.spiegel.de/spiegel/print/d-8002705.html.

Tacitus, Cornelius. *Agricola and the Germania.* Translated by Harold Mattingly. New York: Penguin Classics, 2010.

Tehranian, John. *Whitewashed: America's Invisible Middle Eastern Minority.* New York: NYU Press, 2009.

Theocritus, Tyrtaeus, James Davies, Richard Polwhele, and Matthew James Chapman. *The Idylls of Theocritus, Bion and Moschus and the War-Songs of Tyrtaeus.* Translated by J. Banks and J.M. Chapman. London: H.G. Bohn, 1870.

Thomas, Keith. *Man and the Natural World: Changing Attitudes in England, 1500–1800.* Oxford: Oxford UP, 1996.

Tobler, Alfred. *Kühreihen oder Kühreigen, Jodel und Jodellied in Appenzell.* Leipzig: Hug, 1890.

Tutuola, Amos. *The Palm-Wine Drinkard and My Life in the Bush of Ghosts*. New York: Grove Press, 1993.

"U.K. Approves Human-Animal Hybrids." *Cosmos*, September 6, 2007, www.cosmosmagazine.com/news/1564/uk-approves-human-animal-hybrids.

von Arnim, Achim, and Clemens Brentano. *Des Knaben Wunderhorn: Alte Deutsche Lieder*. Stuttgart: Reclam, 2006.

von Cube, Hellmut. "Die Kühe." *Tierskizzenbüchlein*. Berlin: S. Fischer, 1935: pp. 20–23.

von Tadden, Elisabeth, and Ulrich Schnabel. "Die Kühe haben das Wort. Gene, Tiermehl und andere Mitbürger: Ein Gespräch mit dem Wissenschaftsforscher Bruno Latour." *Die Zeit*, November 30, 2000: pp. 67–68.

von Uexküll, Jakob. *A Foray into the Worlds of Animals and Humans with a Theory of Meaning*. Translated by Joseph D. O'Neil. Minneapolis: University of Minnesota Press, 2010.

Virgil. *The Works of Virgil*, Vol. 2. New York: T&J Swords, 1811.

Weill, Kurt, and Robert Vambery. *Der Kuhhandel: Auszüge*. Königsdorf: Capriccio, 1992.

Xenophanes of Colophon. *Fragments*. Translated by James Lesher. Toronto: University of Toronto Press, 2001.

# IMAGE CREDITS

The numbers on the left refer to page numbers.

9  Aurochs (1556). In Sigismund von Herberstein, *Rerum Moscoviticarum*.
   Basel: Ex Officina Oporiniana, 1571: p. 111.

16  *Contented Cows Give Better Milk* by Bill Catlette and Richard Hadden
    (1998). Contentedcows.com.

25  *A Kingdom for a Cow*, playbill of the London Savoy Theatre (1935)
    © Hein Heckroth.

30  Pantagruel feeding by Gustave Doré (1854). In François Rabelais,
    *The Works of Rabelais*. N.p.: The Bibliophilist Society, 1854.

41  The self-milking cow (1973). In Sri Radhakrishna Sharma, *Tirupati
    Venkatesvara*. Hyderabad: Umashankar Publications, 1973.

42  Weeping cow on the sarcophagus of Queen Kawit (2000 BCE).
    Photo by Eugen Strouhal. In Eugen Stroual, *Life of the Ancient Egyptians*.
    Norman: University of Oklahoma Press, 1996: p. 128.

65  *Dutch Heritage (from Indonesia)* by Jan Cremer (1973) © Jan Cremer/SODRAC
    (2001).

67  Leopard cow © 2001 by Tarzan GmbH.

68  *Eat My Fear* by David Lynch (2000) © Färgfabriken, Stockholm.

73  Man-cow bastard (1556) © Zentralbibliothek Zürich, Graphische
    Sammlung und Fotoarchiv.

97  *The Innocent Eye Test* by Mark Tansey (1981). Oil on canvas. 78 × 120 in.
    (198.1 × 304.8 cm). Partial and Promised Gift of Jan Cowles and Charles

Cowles, in honor of William S. Lieberman, 1988 (1988.183). Image copyright © The Metropolitan Museum of Art / Art Resource, NY.

101 *Rush Hour—Ireland*. Photo by Peter O'Toole © John Hinde Ltd.

125 Balduin Bählamm (1883). In Wilhelm Busch, *Balduin Bählamm, der verhinderte Dichter*, 1883: p. 27.

160 *The Divine Cow*. In Alexandre Piankoff, *The Shrines of Tut-Ankh-Amon*. New York: Pantheon Books, 1955, p. 142.

165 *Le due madri* by Giovanni Segantini (1889) © Comune di Milano—all rights reserved.

189 Officials from Britain's Ministry of Agriculture prepare slaughtered cows for the incinerator in northern England, February 25, 2001, after an outbreak of foot and mouth disease was discovered there. © REUTERS/ Jeff J. Mitchell UK.

191 *Hey Diddle Diddle* by the Brothers Dalziel (1872). In J.W. Elliott, *National Nursery Rhymes and Nursery Songs*. London: George Routledge & Sons, 1872: p. 50.

# ACKNOWLEDGMENTS

WRITING A book about gregarious animals all by oneself would be a rather hope- and cheerless undertaking. My heartfelt thanks for good advice, patient listening, and close reading go to: Dirk Werle-Schneider, Eric Markmiller, Erik Wegerhoff, Heike Geißler, Heinz Drügh, Kerstin Pistorius, Michaela Schäuble, Nadja Sennewald, Nele Schneidereit, Rebecca Lämmle, Stefanie Schlüter, Volker Pantenburg, the *Mittwochsgesellschaft*, Petra Eggers, Thomas Hölzl, Marleen Felius, Shae Clancy and in particular to Anne Wiltafsky and Tobias Bungter. An additional and heartfelt "Dankeschön" for their wonderful work on the English-language edition of this book goes to Doris Ecker and Iva Cheung. Most of all I thank and owe to, as always, Svenja Flaßpöhler.

# INDEX

SVENJA FLAßPÖHLER

FLORIAN WERNER studied American, British, and German literature in both Germany and Scotland and earned his PhD in 2007. His short-story collection *Wir sprechen uns noch* (We still talk) was published in 2005. In 2007, he published *Rapocalypse*, a study of millenarianist hip-hop lyrics, and in 2011 a cultural history of human excrement, *Dunkle Materie: Die Geschichte der Scheiße* (Dark matter: the history of shit). When he is not writing, he tours with his band, Fön, and plays soccer for the German national team of writers, Autonama. He lives with his family in Berlin.

MICHAEL OLSEN

DORIS ECKER is a full-time translator and writer with a BA in Literature and an MA in Linguistics. Pursuing an eclectic career as a researcher, copy editor, linguistic adviser, and bookbinder she has lived and travelled widely in Asia, Europe, and North America. Currently based in Vancouver, Canada, she combines her professional life as a linguist with outdoor activities and frequent travels.